by TOM CARR

Got Grit?

Discover what it takes to GO when the mind and body say NO!

An excellent resource for parents, educators, coaches & youth group leaders

Layout and design by Tonya Daugherty.

Library of Congress Control Number
2007943885

ISBN: 978-1-59850-052-3

10 9 8 7 6 5 4 3 2 1
Printed in the United States

PO Box 115 • Chapin, SC 29036
(800) 209-9774 • (803) 345-1070 • Fax (803) 345-0888
yl@youthlightbooks.com • www.youthlightbooks.com

DEDICATION

To my gritty daughter and son…

Sarah:

Who, during one four-year period, while being married and working full-time for a major fast-food corporation, completed law school.

Aaron:

Who, during one four-year period, while being a full-time teacher and coach, lost 90 pounds and finished the 2007 Boston Marathon in an amazing 3 hours and six minutes.

Will Rogers on "grit"...

This is what he had to say about the runners who participated in C. C. Pyle's foot race across America in 1928. 199 runners started out in California for a 3,422 mile run to New York City. The winner made it in 84 days!

It is the greatest test of stamina and grit that has ever been performed by man. A sporting writer will rave his head off over some football player making an 80-yard run. What would he do if he had to run 80 miles, and do it again the next day, sick, sore feet, bad colds, bum feet, cramps, blisters, no time to lay up and cure 'em, always had to get out in the morning, rain, snow, sleet, desert heat, always be there, ready to go? A marathon that they train for years for is a little over 26 miles. Then they come in and faint, and crowds carry them off. You couldn't faint in this race, nobody to carry you off. If you did, you just laid there, maybe some car run over you, but that was about all you could expect.

Quote by Will Rogers from the book,
C.C. Pyle's Amazing Foot Race,
by Geoff Williams

TABLE OF CONTENTS

PART ONE
GRIT: What Is It? Why Do You Need It?

Preface: Hard Hats, Rope, and Running Shoes 14

Chapter 1: Let the Journey Begin! 17

PART TWO
GRIT: How Do You Get It?

Chapter 2: Getting Along with Others 51

Chapter 3: Responsibility 87

Chapter 4: Integrity 119

Chapter 5: Tenacity 133

PART THREE
GRIT: How Do You Pass It On?

Chapter 6: Passing It on To Others 145

Chapter 7: How to Implement the GOT GRIT?
Program in Your School or Classroom......................157

PART ONE

GRIT:
What Is It?

Why Do You Need It?

PREFACE

Hard hats, rope, and running shoes...

When I began putting together my GOT GRIT? Program, I realized I needed a symbol that projected hard work, determination, getting sweaty, persevering in all kinds of weather, and never using excuses. I chose the yellow hard hat. Think about it; men and women who wear the yellow hard hats while they do their jobs definitely have "grit." They climb power poles to restore electricity in a freezing rain. They lay blacktop in the hot sun. They build houses in the cold of winter and in the heat of summer. These hard hatters work in the dark mines digging coal and they cut down trees in the forest. I hope when my readers think of grit, they'll remember the hard hats, and vice-versa.

Another item that comes to my attention when I think of grit is rope. Mountain climbers grasp rope as they head towards the peak. Helicopters drop rope and rescue people. Children on playgrounds pull with all their strength when they play tug-o-war. Early settlers had to pull up buckets full of water from deep wells. I read of a church that was built high on a mountain in Africa. The church was constructed high up in order to help the parishioners be as close as possible to God and the heavens. The only access to the church was by climbing a rope that hung at the church's entrance. All the parishioners had to be trained in rope climbing. Many climbers, trying to reach the sanctuary, have fallen, broken bones, twisted ankles, fractured skulls, and a few have died as they lost their grip. These people of faith had grit!

Throughout this book you'll see many references to running. I'm a long distance runner. During the past twenty-seven years,

I've logged over 37,000 miles and completed eleven marathons. Running changed my life, physically, mentally, spiritually **and** it helped me acquire grit. As you read this book, I hope you consider choosing a similar activity (you may already have one) that helps you grow in these three areas as well. Whatever the activity, it needs to be something you do almost daily. It should to be something you do alone, so you'll have 'solitude' time. Your special activity could include such things as running, biking, swimming, hiking, walking, aerobics, weight-lifting, yoga, praying, and meditation. As you begin to grow in mind, body, and spirit, you'll be better prepared to master the four components of GRIT* that are explained in this book. My desire is that 1) you'll discover the many personal benefits of having GRIT, and 2) you'll do all you can to help others acquire it, especially our young people.

I struggled for several weeks trying to come up with an appropriate subtitle for this book. I wanted the subtitle to convey the importance of pushing one's self both mentally and physically. Thanks to an article by Cedric Jaggers in the October issue of *Running Journal*, I found what I was looking for. Jaggers wrote, "What is the difference between the good runners and the great runners? It is a fine line that the runner crosses only by having the talent AND then doing the training AND then having the grit to go when the body says no."

Finally, I've attempted to make this book not only a serious working manual, but also a fun read. It is full of short stories, poems, quotes, anecdotes, and bits of humor. People of all ages can benefit from reading this book. Parents will find it helpful as they instill positive character traits in their children. Teachers, counselors, and other educators are provided with a set of guidelines that can be used to set up school-wide GOT GRIT? Programs. The book is a valuable tool for Boy and Girl Scout leaders, coaches, club advisors, and youth groups at church.

To learn more about the GOT GRIT? Program, go to www.gotgrit.org.

—Tom Carr,
October 2007

❖ *Throughout the book if I write the word grit in lower case letters it refers to its generic meaning (hard work, determination, perseverance, etc). When I capitalize the word (GRIT) I'm referring to the four components of my GOT GRIT? Program: **G**etting along with others, **R**esponsibility, **I**ntegrity, and **T**enacity.*

CHAPTER 1
LET THE JOURNEY BEGIN!

Throughout the years I've collected hundreds of true stories of people who had tenacity, perseverance, and who overcame major adversities in their lives. These well-known, and many not-so-well-known, people each had their unique approaches for achieving success. The more I studied these individuals and their amazing stories, the more determined I became to come up with a general term to describe their triumphs. In my search I began to hear the word "grit" being used more and more in the media. On television I would hear ESPN announcers make comments like, "The Philadelphia Eagles are a gritty bunch of players this year." I once heard a local news reporter say, "The victim showed a lot of grit in her struggle against the intruder." Then I read research articles by Angela Duckworth, Martin Seligman, Peter Doskoch, and Carlin Flora that appeared in *Psychology Today* and *Psychological Science*. Their research mentioned the word grit numerous times. Duckworth and Seligman found that self-discipline (grit) is a better predictor of academic success than even IQ. Doskoch and Flora noted, "And yet grit may turn out to be at least as good a gauge of future success as talent itself." They also reported that, "The gritty are more likely to achieve success in school, work, and other pursuits, perhaps because their passion and commitment help them endure the inevitable setbacks that occur in any long-term undertaking."

So I decided to focus on the term grit. In the beginning I utilized the general description of the word grit (hard work, determination, and perseverance). As you'll read later, I added other meanings/components to the word to create my new description: (in capital letters) GRIT. I used it with my students at school where I work as a counselor. I told the young people stories of famous individuals who persevered and overcame adversities. I would tell the students that these people had grit. Then I would ask the students, "Got GRIT?" They would reply, "Yes!" Many would return the question, "Mr. Carr, you got GRIT?"

I encouraged teachers to reinforce my program in the classroom. I placed "GOT GRIT?" posters in the hall. I passed out stickers and plastic yellow hard hats. Every marking period I announced my GRIT Awards. I even named our school mascot, Gritty the Tiger! I began to notice my students putting forth more effort and reducing excuse-making; the program was having a positive impact!

The part of the new program students seemed to enjoy the best **and** remember was my telling of true stories. Following are several brief stories of some of my favorite gritty people that I share with students. I encourage you to pass on these amazing mini biographies to others, especially children.

Rolling Pin Smith: When people today think of the Oregon Trail or the Overland Trail, they think the travelers spent most of the journey riding in covered wagons. Not true. Almost everyone **walked** the 1,932 miles of the Oregon Trail! The wagons were filled with supplies and as the roads got rougher and the horses and cows got weaker, the loads had to be lightened. Precious belongings were discarded along the trail. In his book, *Women & Men on the Overland Trail,* John Faragher tells the story of one gritty traveler in the mid 1840's who had a tough time throwing out one of his valuable personal items.

A man named Smith had a wooden rolling pin that was decided was useless and must be abandoned. I shall never forget how that big man stood there with tears streaming down his face as he said, "Do, I have to throw it away? It was my mother's. I remember she always used it to roll out her biscuits, and they were awful good biscuits." He had to leave it, but they christened him 'Rolling Pin Smith,' a name he carried to the day of his death.

Elsie McLean: In 2007, at the age of 102, she became the oldest golfer ever to make a hole-in-one on a regulation course. Was it luck? Probably not! She told reporters that she still plays 18 holes of golf three days a week.

Three Finger Mordecai Brown: As a young boy growing up in Indiana in the late 1880's, Mordecai loved playing baseball. He was a promising young pitcher but at the age of five he lost one of the fingers on his throwing hand in a piece of farm machinery. A year later he broke another finger on the same hand while chasing a pig. The finger never healed properly. He still had a dream of making it to the big leagues. Even though he had only three "good" fingers on his throwing hand, he spent many hours a day strengthening his fingers by squeezing rocks, fruit, and balls. His three-fingered hand was stronger than most people's five-fingered hands. Because of the unusual grip he had on the baseball, when he threw it, it moved around so much that it was almost impossible to hit. His uniqueness got him to the major leagues as a pitcher. He won 272 games and made it into the prestigious Baseball Hall of Fame.

Abebe Bikila: Abebe was the son of a shepherd and raised in poverty in Ethiopia. He had the gift of running long distances even though he never owned a pair of running shoes. He qualified to run the marathon (26.2 miles) in the 1960 Olympics in Rome. He showed up at the starting line with no shoes! Some of the other runners chuckled and made rude comments. Despite running barefoot, he won the gold medal! Four years later he won another gold medal at the Tokyo Olympics. This time he wore shoes!

Crazy Horse: This great Lakota warrior survived many battles, but he is more often remembered by Native Americans for his modesty and shyness. He refused to participate in the Lakota ritual *wahtoglakapi* in which fighting men would share their exploits and acts of heroism on the battlefield.

James Curry: James was a slave in North Carolina in the early 1880's. At that time many slaves were not allowed to read, but James was determined to do so, even though he knew he would be severely punished if caught with a book in his possession. How did he learn? He got very creative. In the book, *Self-Taught*, Heather Andrea Williams quotes Curry from his narrative, "When my master's family were all gone away on the Sabbath, I used to go into the house and get down the great Bible, and lie down on the piazza and read, taking care, however, to put it back before they returned."

J.K. Rowling: Almost every young person is familiar with the *Harry Potter* book series. Rowling, the author, eventually became the wealthiest woman in England. She dreamed of being a writer but a difficult divorce left her practically penniless in 1993. She and her baby girl moved to Scotland where they lived in a small, poorly-furnished apartment and survived on a meager supplement from the government. Broke, hungry, and cold, Rowling would bundle up her daughter and head to the coffee shop. While her baby slept in a carriage next to her table, J.K. would drink a cup of coffee. She nursed the drink as long as she could because she didn't want to return to her cold apartment. While sitting there she would take out a pencil and write stories on a napkin. Her first *Harry Potter* book originated while drinking coffee in the warm shop.

Scott Laio: The June 3, 2005 issue of *Sports Illustrated* told the tale of this remarkable young man. He died of apparent heart failure at the age of 20 as he and his Boston College rowing team crossed the finish line in first place at the Dad Vail Regatta in Philadelphia. Rowing is one of the hardest sports. Participants must "give it all" and work as a team in order to compete successfully. Scott gave everything he had at the D.V. Regatta! Totally exhausted he collapsed in the boat. The magazine article noted, "His death happened in front of his father, who was watching from the shore, but I like to think that a moment before he left us, Scott experienced a feeling perhaps understood fully only by those who have utterly exhausted themselves in the pursuit of an athletic goal." Scott had grit!

Aunt Arlene: Along the Blue Ridge Parkway in North Carolina, there is an old building known as Puckett Cabin. The log structure was the home of Aunt Arlene in the early 1800's. She traveled to hundreds of isolated cabins as a midwife. Meanwhile she had twenty-four children herself but none lived past infancy. She died at the age of 102.

Maxey Flier: Maxey graduated from law school at the age of thirty-six and took the bar exam for the first time. He didn't pass, but he kept trying. He took it again, and again, and again but couldn't pass. Finally on the forty-eighth try, he passed. At the age of sixty-eight he officially became a lawyer.

Jean-Dominique Bauby: He suffered a rare stroke to the brain stem. Only his left eye and brain escaped damage. Despite this tragedy, he was able to write a best-seller, *The Diving Bell and the Butterfly*. He was able to write the book by operating his special computer with the blinking of his left eye!

Wilma Rudolph: Wilma was raised in poverty with her twenty-one brothers and sisters. At the age of four, she was struck with pneumonia and scarlet fever, which left her paralyzed in one of her legs. She was unable to walk for a long period of time and had to wear leg braces. She eventually recovered and went on to become the fastest female runner in the world in 1960. Also in 1960, she won three gold medals in the Olympics.

Andrew Wiles: When Andrew was ten years old, he first heard of Fermat's Last Theorem, a seemingly simple math problem that had puzzled mathematicians for 350 years. He 'played' with it for a while, trying to solve it. Then he abandoned the problem for several years. He decided to try to solve it again. He did! He estimated it took him over 15,000 hours over several years. He became famous and was named as one of *People* magazine's 25 Most Intriguing People of the Year.

Shawn Hessee: Shawn is one of my best friends. He helps to keep me inspired and motivated. He was born with cerebral palsy and has almost no control over his legs. He has spent most of his life in a wheelchair. In middle school, he became interested in wrestling. People questioned his decision to go out for the team. "Shawn, how can you wrestle without walking, running, or standing?" He was determined. He never missed practice, worked hard, and became a vital part of his teams in middle and high school. Shawn had a perfect won-loss record. He wrestled 88 matches, and lost every one! Currently Shawn travels the county as a motivational speaker.

Missy Foy: Missy is another friend of mine and a fellow runner. In the summer of 2007 she ran hundreds of miles in preparation for the National Fifty-Mile Championships. On race day she got off to a good start until the 20-mile mark. In her email to me she wrote, "Then, a car flew over a ridge heading toward me and I moved to the right side of the trail. A deer, standing at the edge of the forest, bolted into the road, nailed me on the right side, and sliced the back of my right heel with one of its hooves!

In trying not to fall down, I pulled my left quad. I heard the deer slide on the dirt and gravel behind me and then run back into the forest." Although she was sore and bleeding, she ran the remaining thirty miles and was the second place finisher in the women's division!

Charles Schwab: Charles is one of the best known, respected businessmen in the country. He founded one of the biggest discount brokerages in the world, despite having dyslexia. Although he struggled with math and reading in school, he worked hard, accepted no excuses, graduated, and started his own successful business. This wealthy man now gives his time and money helping young people learn how to read.

Cal Ripken, Jr.: Cal earned the nickname, "Iron Man" because he went sixteen years in a row without missing a game for his Baltimore Orioles. He played in 2,632 consecutive games! Bumps, bruises, twisted ankles, sprains, illness, rain, snow, heat, and other distractions never stopped him from fielding his position.

Rosa Parks: Is there anyone who doesn't know about Rosa? This woman exemplifies grit. She helped change the world that one day when she refused to give up her seat on a bus to a white person.

Rick Warren: Rick is the author of one of the best-selling books ever, *The Purpose-Driven Life*. He told the *New Yorker* magazine, "I'm not a good writer, I'm a pastor." He lets others know that he has ADHD (Attention Deficit-Hyperactivity Disorder) and how difficult it was to "force" himself to sit for long periods of time to write the book. He locked himself in his office, twelve hours every day for seven months to complete the manuscript. He said, "I would get up at four-thirty, arrive at my special office at five, and I would write from five to five.

I'm a people person and it about killed me to be alone." He had to make several sacrifices but it paid off. Millions of dollars poured in. He and his wife decided to do a reverse-tithe. They keep ten percent and give ninety percent to the church.

Bill Monroe: He is known as the Father of Bluegrass Music. Bill Monroe and Johnny Cash are the only two artists to be members of these three institutions: Country Music Hall of Fame, International Bluegrass Music Hall of Fame, and the Rock and Roll Hall of Fame. Bill had grit right up to the end of his life. When one of his closest friends, singer John Hartford, visited him in the hospital a few days before he died at the age of eighty-five, he was smiling. John asked him about the smile, and Monroe replied, "Hey, I've got a couple new songs in my head; they're going to be good." So, even though he knew he was dying, he was still writing songs.

Mary Ann Evans: She was an English novelist during the 1800's. Back in that era, it was almost impossible for a woman to get her writings published so she used the pen name, George Eliot. By changing her name she was able to get many books and poems published. My favorite quote from her is, "What do we live for if not to make life less difficult for each other."

Katherine Switzer: She was a great American marathoner during the 1960's and 70's. She was a pioneer for women's long distance running. In the early days of marathoning women were not allowed to compete. It was believed to be a "man's sport" because a 26.2 mile race was too dangerous for women. Before 1967, no women were allowed to run the Boston Marathon. That year, she registered as "K. V. Switzer," so no one knew she was a woman. She stuffed her long hair under her hat, put on her race number and took off. Halfway through the run a race official spotted her and tried to push her off the road, but she continued and finished. From that year on, more and more women have competed in marathons.

Bob May: As a child, Bob was often teased and bullied because he was small and frail. Later in life, he turned his bad experiences into something positive. He wrote the lyrics to one of the most popular Christmas songs ever. It told the story of an animated animal character that was teased. The song was, *Rudolph the Red-Nosed Reindeer*.

Stephen Reed: Stephen, a family practice physician, has not missed a day of running in over thirty years! What makes his streak even more remarkable is that he runs a minimum of three miles, every day, outdoors in Maine!

Jamie Foxx: Many young people today watch Jamie on television and in the movies, and they listen to his music and think how "lucky" he is to be so famous and rich. Yes, he has sold millions of records, had his own television show, and won Academy Awards, but his road to success was not all luck. When he was 7 months old, his parents abandoned him; they gave him to his grandmother to raise. Jamie thought his grandmother was mean because she made him practice piano, go to church, and participate in Boy Scouting. She wouldn't let him hang out with other boys in the streets. He was a great high school football player. Even though his father still lived in the same town, he **never** went to see his son play! Despite early setbacks in life, Jamie Foxx found success.

Billy Mills: Billy grew up as a poor child on the Pine Ridge Indian Reservation in South Dakota. Thanks to his running ability, he got a scholarship to college and eventually joined the United States Marines. He desired to participate in the 1964 Olympics in Tokyo. After training for only eighteen months, in only his sixth 10,000 meter run of his life, he stunned the world in what is called the greatest upset in Olympic history when he won the gold medal! Billy is a very spiritual man as you can see from these two quotes. Here is what he wrote in his diary prior to winning the gold medal, "God has given me the ability, the rest is up to me. Believe. Believe. Believe." At another time, he said, "My life is a gift to me from my Creator. What I do with my life is my gift back to the Creator."

Hank Aaron: Aaron was my boyhood hero. I named my son after him. Many sports fans consider him the greatest home run hitter of all time. In 1974, he passed the great Babe Ruth by hitting his 715th home run. Although he accomplished that great feat, he nearly lost his life. Many people are not aware of the adversity he overcame on the path to passing the Babe. Back in the 1970's there were many racist people who did not want a young black man topping the great white baseball hero, Babe Ruth. Here are a few examples of Aaron's struggles as he neared the record:

❖He received thousands of threatening letters such as this one, "You are not going to break the record established by the great Babe Ruth if I can help it… my gun will be watching your every black move."

❖As he neared the record, Aaron told his teammates, for their safety, not to sit next to him in the dugout in case someone tried to shoot him. As a sign of support, his teammates continued to sit next to him.

❖During the chase to the record, Aaron had a 24-hour bodyguard. He stayed in separate hotels from his fellow players. He was told not to venture out alone and had to have his food secretly delivered to his room.

Ashrita Furman: As of July 2007, he has broken more than 150 Guinness World Records. Some of his more unique records include: apple bobbing, rope skipping on stilts, underwater Hula Hooping, lemon eating (fastest to peel and eat a lemon, 19.97 seconds), forward rolls, deep knee bends, grape catching, sit ups, hopping on one leg, basketball dribbling (97 miles), somersaults. and jumping jacks (45,027).

Dale Hanson: In 2007, he retired from being a school bus driver in Iowa for 61 years! Now that took a lot of grit!

Jack Prelutsky: He was awarded the first ever "Children's Poet Laureate" by the Chicago-based Poetry Foundation. His poetry books have sold more than a million copies and are enjoyed by millions of children. One of his most popular book characters is *Bananaconda*, a cross between a boa constrictor and banana. Jack was raised in a poor working-class family in New York and started writing poetry at the age of 22. To make ends meet, he drove cabs, picked fruit, built loft beds, taught guitar and performed in coffee houses and clubs. He borrowed money and took several risks before finally getting published. The breakthrough of his career came in 1984 with the publication of *New Kid on the Block*. My favorite Prelutsky poem is *Homework! Oh Homework!*

HOMEWORK! OH HOMEWORK!

Homework! Oh homework!

I hate you! You stink!

I wish I could wash you

away in the sink,

if only a bomb

would explode you to bits.

Homework! Oh homework!

You're giving me the fits!

GRIT & TRUE GRIT

As I continued to develop my *GOT GRIT?* Program, I felt there was still something missing. Then along came Zach Johnson. In the spring of 2007, Zach won the Masters Golf Tournament in Augusta, Georgia. The Masters is considered the most prestigious golf tournament in the United States. The winner gets to wear the famous "green jacket," receive a huge cash award and get many endorsements. Almost overnight Zach Johnson became a big time sports hero. A reporter asked him how he would like to be remembered. He responded, "I'd like to be remembered as a good guy, someone that everybody wants to hang around with, a guy who's gritty and never gives up." BINGO! His comments helped me fill in the missing piece. I began to realize that some people have grit (tenacity, perseverance,) but they may lack certain character traits (kindness, compassion, integrity). In other words, some people have grit, while others have what I call (my apologies to John Wayne) true grit.

I had to add some new components to my program. I had to develop a set of guidelines to help people acquire true grit. Having tenacity, perseverance, determination, and overcoming adversities was not enough; people also need to, as Zach Johnson noted, be a "good guy."

Throughout history there have been many cruel leaders, dictators, kings, and conquerors that had grit. No one can deny that evil people such as Hitler, Sadaam Hussian, and Genghis Khan were tenacious. They were persistent, had goals, never gave up, worked hard every day, and spent hours planning their strategies, but they lacked true grit. They killed thousands, attacked innocent people, destroyed villages, neglected their own families, lied, cheated, stole, abused people and lacked compassion and tolerance. Consider these remarks by the vicious conqueror, Genghis Khan, "The greatest joy a man can have in victory: to conquer one's enemy's armies, to pursue them, to deprive them of their possessions, to reduce their families to tears, to ride on their horses, and to make love to their wives and daughters." Thankfully these evil people always fail. Gandhi said, "When I despair, I remember that all through history, the way of truth and love always won. There have been murderers and tyrants, and for a time they can seem invincible. But in the end they always fail. Think of it, always."

As a counselor I've worked with young people, married couples, and athletes. Many of my clients had one aspect of grit; they had tenacity. They set goals and did all they could to reach their goals, but along the way they neglected their families and other responsibilities. There are many men and women who spend almost all their time and energy on their occupations. They work long hours seeking promotions or trying to set sales records, but along the way they soon find that their marriages and children suffer. I've read several biographies of Olympic athletes who won gold medals but "lost" their spouses.

Eventually I added the missing components to my program. I took each letter of the word grit and added a brief description after each one. If people closely follow these four steps, they'll have 'true grit.'

G   *Getting along with others (social skills)*

R   *Responsibility (to family, community, church, country, learning, health, nutrition, fitness)*

I   *Integrity (honesty, kindness, compassion, sincerity)*

T   *Tenacity (perseverance, determination)*

Evil rulers, selfish spouses, and vain athletes often posses the T (tenacity), but not the G-R-I. They fall. People with true grit posses all four components and they tend to be happy, successful members of society.

GRIT: THEN & NOW

As adults, we have more control over our fate than do young people. We have more control over our diet, exercise, responsibilities, earnings, and involvement in our community and religious institutions, but so many of our young people today lack the basic skills and tools in order to master the four steps of the GRIT Program. They need our love, patience, inspiration, and quality time. They need positive adult role models in their lives (coaches, teachers, parents, pastors) who will show, and teach, them how to get along with others, become responsible, have integrity, and be tenacious. One of the most important aspects of the GRIT Program is this: Adults must acquire grit themselves and then pass it on to others, especially our youth. **We can't pass on GRIT if we don't have any!**

Years ago adults and children needed grit just to survive. Families had to cut trees, build cabins, grow a garden, care for animals, go hunting and fishing, and walk long distances to school, church, and the general store. Nowadays, is life too easy for children? Think about it. In most homes children have televisions, computers, video games, cell phones, micro-wave ovens, heat, air-conditioning and food in the refrigerator. Many kids seldom leave the comfort of their homes. Also, I have had bunches of parents tell me, because of advances in technology, that there fewer and fewer chores to be assigned. Life appears to be great for a vast majority of today's youth!

ARE WE GUILTY?

I would venture to say that most parents and teachers agree that our young people need more GRIT, but are they, and other adults, guilty of making life too easy for kids? Are they giving children too many chances and choices? Are they providing too many nets to catch their children and students when they fall? I believe many of us are guilty! During the past few years I've been gathering many interesting bits of information from newspapers, journal articles, websites, and books to prove that many adults are, in fact, hindering our children's progress to master the four steps of the GRIT Program. When you read the following list, ask yourself, "Are these things helping or hurting our children?"

❖ Teachers are being encouraged to stop using red colored pens and markers to grade papers. The color 'red' denotes failure and may cause children to feel bad. Instead, teachers are being encouraged to use soothing, more calming colors such as purple.

❖ Many kindergarten teachers no longer use 'smiley faces' and 'frowny faces' to grade their students. 'Frowny faces' can make little kids feel bad. Instead, the teachers use the more passive terms, 'smiley faces' and 'un-smiley faces.'

❖ In many schools today they do not say that a child has failed; they say he is 'success-delayed.' And, their 'at-risk' students are now referred to as, 'on the verge of success' students.

❖ More and more "experts" are coming up with new labels for children. In one of his weekly newspaper columns, family psychologist, John Rosemond vented his frustration with an article in the August, 2007 issue of *Parents Magazine* that suggested a few new, (more positive?) labels for children. The article said we shouldn't call kids *shy*, call them *careful*. Don't label kids as *fussy*, call them *selective*. The one label that angered Rosemond and me the most was the use of the term *stubborn*. The article suggested we use the term *tenacious* instead. Rosemond says, "No." He writes, "Tenacious means the determination to try and try and try again until one succeeds. Stubborn means obstinate, immovable. My oldest child was both stubborn and tenacious, but they are not the same thing. His stubbornness was infuriating, while his tenacity was the source of paternal pride."

* Numerous schools have eliminated playground games such as tag and dodge ball because players 'get out,' and that can hurt their self-esteem.

* One newspaper article told the story of a couple pre-schools that no longer play the game of musical chairs because, heaven forbid, when the music stops, one player won't have a chair to sit in!

* On some playgrounds they no longer play 'tug-o-war'; they play 'tug-o-peace.'

* Our playgrounds have been dulled. Tall slides, see-saws, monkey bars, and merry-go-rounds are rarely seen. A CBS news report noted, "Schoolyards and neighborhood parks have been transformed over the past two decades in the name of safety and in fear of lawsuits. The old standbys have given way to shorter, guardrail-lined plastic-and-steel play structures, leaving childhood experts complaining about cookie-cutter sameness and sterile designs that do not challenge today's youngsters."

* No more tree-climbing? Many of us had a great time climbing trees when we were young. Now, because children are not outdoors as much, or because of over-protective parents, we seldom see kids in trees. A major study in England (2007) noted, "It may be better for the occasional child to fall out of a tree and break their wrist than develop RSI (repetitive strain injury) from playing computer games." The study also reported, "Figures obtained from England's hospitals show the number of tree-related accidents has fallen by 36 percent from 1999-2006."

❖ Young children need to get outdoors and play every day, but many get off the bus with oodles of homework. A five or six year-old has already spent six or seven hours in school. Should he have to sit at a desk at home every evening and do more work? Homework is a very sedentary activity and is it really that useful for elementary students? In the September 24, 2006 issue of *The New York Daily News*, an article noted, "According to a 2006 Duke University review of 180 studies, there is almost zero correlation between homework and achievement in elementary school, and only a minor correlation in middle school."

❖ Some physical education teachers have kids juggling scarves instead of balls. Scarves are easier to catch and cause children less frustration.

❖ Many schools incorporate a program called New Games. These games encourage students to work together to achieve a goal. There is no real competition, and in the games, no one keeps score. Teamwork and not keeping score are okay at times. But what is wrong with a little competition? When children grow up they have to compete to get into college, make the varsity volleyball team, and to get a job.

❖ Author Sally Satel, M.D., in her book, *One Nation under Therapy*, notes, "In 2001, the Girl Scouts of America introduced a "Stress Less Badge," for girls eight to eleven. It featured an embroidered hammock suspended from two green trees. According to the *Junior Girl Scout Badge Book*, girls earn the award by practicing 'focused-breathing,' creating a stress-less kit, or keeping a feelings diary.' I don't disagree with the fact some young girls are stressed, but won't having to earn **another** badge cause more stress?

- ❖ What about Honor Rolls? Many schools are no longer putting their Honor Rolls in the local newspapers. Why? Shouldn't students who work hard get some recognition? Has any child been 'traumatized' because her name wasn't in the paper? By not having her name in the paper, will that motivate her to work harder? Sometimes I think the Honor Rolls are more important to the parents than the students; they want to see **their** kid's name in the paper! In the past, students had to get all A's to make the Honor Roll. Then it was changed to the A, B Honor Roll; a student had to get at least a B in every subject. Now some schools allow a child on the Honor Roll if they have a B average. In other words, little Lucy could get 3 A's and 3 C's and be on the Honor Roll!

- ❖ iPods for high test scores? One high school in North Carolina announced that students who get the highest possible score on a state-mandated writing test would earn more than just a proud pat on the back and enhanced self-esteem. The school would give students who earn a "4" on the test a new iPod, a portable music and video player.

- ❖ I've been finding reports that many schools are now giving students a second set of books so they don't have to carry the heavy objects back and forth. Now they can't use the excuse, "I forgot my books." How is this helping children to become more responsible?

- ❖ Recently there has been a big push to implement Character Education programs in our schools. Do children need to learn such traits as honesty, respect, trust, perseverance, etc.? Of course! But should they receive tangible reinforcers for following the traits? Do we want Mary opening the door for someone because a) she knows it is the right thing to do, or b) she is doing it so she'll receive a reward? Harvard professor and education expert, Alfie Kohn has done numerous studies on

Character Education programs. He's discovered that such programs in schools do, in fact, encourage students to have more character; they will behave better. But the research also finds that most children are behaving better to get the goodies. Once the goodies are no longer being handed out, many of the students revert back to old behaviors. Here is a perfect example from the USA TODAY, July 6, 2007, "In Pennsylvania, researchers went so far to give prizes to school children who ate fruits and vegetables. That worked while the prizes were offered, but when the researchers came back seven months later, when the prizes were no longer being offered, the kids had reverted to their original eating habits: soda and chips." In other words, many kids are doing "the right thing," not because it's the right thing to do, but because they'll get something. Schools are giving away t-shirts, ice cream, stickers, candy, pizza, and tokens for kids caught being good. I want my students picking up a piece of trash on the playground because they know littering is wrong, not because they might receive a sticker. As adults, we don't always get goodies for doing the right thing. When you pick up a piece of trash at the local park, does the park ranger run up to you and say, "Thanks for picking up the trash. Here's a coupon for a free ice cream at the Dairy Queen!"?

❖ Not all our children are proficient in math or reading but many are proficient at complaining. In his book, *The Progress Paradox*, Gregg Easterbrook introduces us to the term 'complaint proficiency.' As a whole, many adults and children in today's society are getting pretty good at complaining. How are we doing as role models in this area? Are we always blaming others for our plight? Are we growing a generation of complainers who won't accept responsibility for their actions? Are you accommodating children who say things like, *I'm bored. It's too cold to go out. Is this all we have to eat?*

My television doesn't get HBO. It's the teacher's fault; she didn't explain it well. I don't like the coach; he makes us run too much.?

❖ Many children today have a problem-solving deficit. We are often guilty of helping them too much when they encounter difficult/challenging dilemmas. Because of the emphasis on math and reading in school, students are getting less science and social studies. If taught properly, those two subjects assist our children greatly in creativity which, in turn, helps in problem-solving. A 2007 report in *TIME* magazine shows that during the last five years, elementary students are getting 23 fewer minutes of science each week and 17 fewer minutes of social studies.

❖ Children today are being raised in a 'Pinocchio Culture' where they see and hear politicians, athletes, parents, educators, and even religious leaders lying, cheating, and stealing. Is there a 'Pinocchio Culture' in your home?

❖ According to *USA TODAY*, June 25, 2007, "Currently one-third of U.S. children and teens, about 25 million kids, are either overweight or obese." What are we doing in our homes and schools to address the obesity issue? How can our children have GRIT if they are unhealthy? It is quite obvious, kids need to eat better and exercise more. They need to get outside, but are we scaring them to the point they hesitate to leave the house? When children constantly see missing kids' pictures on milk cartons, watch Amber Alerts on television, observe CNN or FOX News shows about kidnappings or abductions, it's no wonder they seldom venture outside. We even have the local weather man warning us not to go outside because it's too hot! I don't remember staying inside when I was young because it was hot out! Folks, it is no more dangerous outside today than it was fifty years ago. Be sure to read my list of reasons why children are safer outdoors than they are inside in Chapter 3.

❖ Are we pushing too much technology on our children too soon? Have you noticed that kids aren't naming their dogs Bowzer anymore, they are naming them Browzer! I personally don't think students should touch a computer in school until second or third grade. They need to focus on social skills, fine and gross motor skills, reading, handwriting, art, and music. Here's another question to ponder. Are computers in school really helping children learn? Consider these headlines from newspapers and journal articles in the last few years:

$14 Million Study Proves Student Laptops Ineffective Academically

Why Computers Have Not Saved the Classroom

Computers in Class Are Lousy Teachers

Laptop Computers Creating King-Sized Illusion for State

Contrary to Expectations: Computers Don't Necessarily Improve Students' Writing

Computers in Schools: High Technology Doesn't Equal High Achievement

❖ What about health issues related to computers? According to a survey involving 649 undergraduate and postgraduate students in 2007 by the University College of London, 57% of respondents had experienced aches (neck, back, shoulder, and/or wrist) as a result of their laptop use.

❖ Young people are reading too much fiction. Sometimes I think they read so much fiction that they have trouble distinguishing between what is real and what isn't.

Columnist, Will Fitzhugh, says, "It is clearer and clearer that most high school students, when they read a book, read fiction. The College Board's Reading List of 101 Books for College-Bound Students includes only three works of non-fiction." I believe children can be inspired more by true stories.

❖ I once had a principal say to me, "Tom, make sure everybody gets an award." I wanted to say, "Even Jacob, he hasn't done a lick of work this marking period, plus he's been suspended twice!" I'm strongly in favor of rewarding kids when it has been earned, but I think schools, coaches, and some youth group leaders pass out too many awards for minimal effort. For example, twenty years ago if the local Little League team won a championship, the team would get one trophy to place on the coach's mantle at home. Then, a few years later if the team finished first, they would get a championship team trophy and all the players would get a medal or small trophy. Nowadays it seems **everyone** walks away with a medal, trophy, plaque, or certificate. Even Jacob! He was on the last place team; he got kicked out of two games; he back-talked to the coach, missed several practices, and would sit down in the outfield when angry. But, he got his trophy! Young people need recognition, but let it be truly deserved!

❖ We are raising a generation of "praise junkies." Over the years parents and teachers have been conditioned to praise often. But could too much praise be detrimental? Richard Benyo, editor of *Marathon & Beyond*, expressed his frustration over "too much praise" when writing about some of today's runners. He notes, "Some runners expect to run well on more rest than training. Runners who train little but expect decent results have spent too much time in the modern school system where everyone who shows up gets a gold star. Or if you show up late but not quite as late as last week, you are praised and rewarded. Or if you merely exist, you expect praise." Recent research encourages us to praise a child's effort, not his/her intelligence. In his book, *Punished by Rewards*, Alfie Kohn sites four "problems with praise."

—When someone is praised for succeeding at tasks that aren't terribly difficult, he may take this to mean he isn't very smart: that must be why someone had to praise him. This inference leads to low expectations of success at difficult tasks, which may in turn result in decreased persistence and performance intensity at these tasks.

—Telling someone how good she is can increase the pressure she feels to live up to the compliment.

—While Skinner declared that praise "encourages us to take the risks that expand our lives," there is reason to think that exactly the opposite often occurs. One classic classroom study, by Mary Budd Rowe, found that elementary school students whose teachers frequently used praise showed less task persistence than their peers.

—Finally, praise, like other rewards, often undermines the intrinsic motivation that leads people to do their best.

❖ Schools are falsely labeling millions of students as "proficient." Because of the No Child Left Behind initiative, each of the fifty states is required to develop its own state test to determine proficiency. Of course each state wants their state to look good by having a high percentage of proficient students, which means the bar for passing is often set very low. In many states, students need to get approximately only one out of four multiple-choice questions correct to be considered eligible for promotion to the next grade. That's right, if they get one out of four correct, they are considered proficient! Students think they are proficient; parents think their kids are proficient, when they really aren't. Several states are guilty of even more deception. Mississippi, for instance, in 2005 showed that almost 90% of their fourth grade students (according their state test) were proficient in reading, while the National Assessment of Educational Progress (a federal government standardized test) found that less than twenty percent of Mississippi fourth graders were proficient in reading! (*Time*, June 4, 2007). Because of the NCLB, testing seems to take priority over other important things such as creativity and social skills. Respected education author and Yale professor, Dr. James Comer stated in a 2006 interview, "What we're going to have soon—unless we pay more attention—is prisoners with high test scores."

❖ Finally, I couldn't finish this section without mentioning 'helicopter parenting.' Although authors Jim Fay and Foster Cline were the first to write about it over twenty years ago, I swear I hear the term used more now than ever! Helicopters tend to "hover and rescue." Many parents today hover above their children and rescue them, not wanting their little darlings to suffer any negative consequences. If we want our children to grow up to be responsible people, we can't keep bailing them out when they get in trouble. One of the best things we can do for children is to let them fall; let them fail once in a while. They need to learn how to handle things on their own. I remember as a child getting upset with my father when he wouldn't always run to my rescue. Whenever I came home from school to complain about a bully or mean teacher, he would always say two things, "I'm sorry," and "What are **you** going to do about it?"

OFF TO THE LAND OF GRIT

Before you lace up your running shoes or hiking boots and strap on your backpacks to begin your personal journey to the *Land of GRIT,* let's review a few things.

What is GRIT? Having GRIT involves mastering the following four components:

        G- Getting along with others
        R- Responsibility
        I- Integrity
        T- Tenacity

When these four things are mastered, one has 'true' GRIT. Don't forget, it is possible for some people to have only tenacity, but without the other three components, they'll never be truly happy and successful.

Why do you need it? You need GRIT for three reasons; self-improvement, to help make the world a better place, and to be able to pass it on to others. Martin Luther King, Jr. reminds us, "Every man must decide whether he will walk in the creative light of altruism or the darkness of destructive selfishness. This is the judgment. Life's persistent and most urgent question is, 'What are you doing for others?'"

Toto, Dorothy, and her three friends nervously began an adventure to find the *Land of Oz*, hoping that when they got there, their lives would be changed for the better. I feel very confident that **your life** will change when your journey ends in the *Land of GRIT.* What can you expect to encounter on your travels?

Don't expect this! Your trip will be quick and easy. The road will be flat and shaded by beautiful trees. The weather will always be sunny and warm. All along the way there will be soft, comfortable benches where you can rest a bit. Birds will be singing and butterflies floating by. Crowds will line the road to cheer you on! Children will hand you cool bottles of water, fresh fruit, and chocolate candy. You won't have to worry about getting lost because guides will point you in the right direction. When you reach your destination a large, cheering crowd will greet you. An orchestra will be playing music as the mayor drapes a large medal around your neck. A newspaper reporter will take your picture and write an article for the next edition. Everyone will look up to you. You'll be a hero!

What to expect! Your trip will be long and difficult. The road isn't smooth and flat; in fact, most of the time you'll have to ascend many hills. Almost every day the weather will be terrible. Sometimes you'll have to slush through snow and mud, and once in a while you'll get lost. You won't find many people along the way to cheer you on, and the few who do show up may hassle, criticize, and/or ridicule you; they'll question your motives. You better pack your own food and drinks. When you reach the *Land of GRIT* you won't find any cheering crowds, bands playing, or someone passing out medals. Your picture and story won't reach the media. But, guess what? You'll feel **great** and you'll be proud of your accomplishment; you worked hard! Also, now that you've got GRIT you realize how important it is to pass it on to others and you are excited about doing it.

NOW FOR SOME GOOD NEWS!

You can start your journey right now! Anne Frank said, "How wonderful it is that nobody needs to wait a single moment before starting to improve the world." Yes, start now! You don't need to attend a meeting, go to an in-service, participate in team-building activities, form a committee, or draw-up some paperwork. I believe much valuable human time is wasted on these things. So many people wait for group approval or guidance before making changes. Yes, there are a few "must" gatherings we should attend, but some of the best changes, findings, discoveries, and inventions have occurred with what is called the *Eureka! Factor*. Paul Paulus, a psychologist with the University of Texas at Arlington's Group Creativity Lab, has been researching the art of brainstorming, which is used often in meetings and committees. He found that group brainstorming really doesn't work well. In fact, business owners and leaders are almost always better off instructing employees to brainstorm individually. Individuals may be working in their gardens, driving their cars, or out walking when great ideas come to them and they shout out, "Eureka!" Most of my creative thoughts have occurred while out running, not while attending lengthy meetings, conferences, or workshops.

Following are a few opinions on paperwork, meetings, team-building, and committees. Hopefully after reading these you'll consider taking a risk or two, by-passing some of them, and progressing on your own. For example, my principal approached me about the high number of children who arrived by car each morning who were tardy. She asked me to see what I could do to decrease the number of "tardies." I could have formed a committee! I would have had to invite several teachers and parents to join the committee, schedule dates and times, got some chart tablets to hang on the wall for our brainstorming sessions, purchase some colored markers, make a list of recommendations, print committee results in the newsletter, and so on! By the time all that got finished, three more months would have passed and our tardy problem would have still been an issue.

Instead, while out running, I had a *Eureka Moment!* I went out and bought three flags; one yellow, one green, and one red. The next day I started hanging out the green flag so parents could see it. Green flag meant parents were dropping their kids off on time. With five minutes before the starting bell rang, I hung up the yellow flag, letting parents know that time was running short. When the bell rang, I hung up the red flag letting parents and children know that they were tardy. Thanks to this simple intervention, "tardies" dropped by almost 50% the remainder of the year.

Paperwork:

"Paperwork is the embalming fluid of bureaucracy, maintaining an appearance of life where none exists."
—Anonymous

"A memorandum is written not to inform the reader but to protect the writer."
—Dean Acheson

Meetings:

"If you had to identify, in one word, the reason why the human race has not achieved, and never will achieve its full potential, that word would be 'meetings.'"
—anonymous.

Team-Building:

After nearly thirty years in business and education, it still amazes me how much money corporations and schools pay consultants to conduct team-building activities that involve such things as building foam-rubber towers, stacking blocks, juggling, "warm fuzzy" games and solving puzzles. Sometimes clowns, magicians, and comedians are brought in. Rarely have I seen positive long-term changes in productivity and morale after the consultants left town. I remember the time my son, a middle school teacher, returned from a week-long teacher in-service/training program. I asked him about it. He told me that his fellow faculty members spent most of the time arguing and 'talking about each other.' He said, "They were more upset with each other after the conference than before." I inquired, "What was the focus of the conference?" He replied, "Team-building."

Committees:

"A committee is an animal with four back legs."
—John LeCarre

"If you wish to avoid a decision, either send out a memo, or set up a committee to conduct an in-depth study."
—*Epson's Complete Office Companion*

"A committee is a cul-de-sac down which ideas are lured and then quietly strangled."
—Barnett Cocks

"Committee: A group of people who individually can do nothing, but as a group decide that nothing can be done."
—Fred Allen

Schools and churches are inundated with committees! How many have you served on? Writer and humorist, C. McNair Wilson pokes a little fun at committees in his book, *Everyone Wants to Go to Heaven, but...*

Wally Peat, Church Bus Driver for First Church downtown was fired last Monday for yelling at Melody Naramore and making her cry. It seems that Melody had her head out the window-again-and was spitting into the open, driver's-side windows of passing autos. Though the church agreed with Wally that Melody's behavior was inappropriate and dangerous, they did not concur with Mr. Peat's chosen method of discipline. He stopped the bus, walked back to where Melody was expectorating, and shouted, "Sit down, you little fart!" An announcement was placed in the church bulletin the following Sunday. "Until a permanent replacement can be hired, the church bus will be driven by associate pastor, Ed Holt, beginning this Sunday." Melody had her bus privileges rescinded for thirty days, pending a thorough review by the Committee on Church Bus Behavior and Maintenance.

It's time to get up and take action. I have a special self-motivator. It comes from a church marquee that was promoting an upcoming sermon, ARE WE STANDING ON THE PROMISES OR JUST SITTING ON THE PREMISES?

I'll finish this chapter with one of my favorite stories of a gritty individual. It is about a remarkable man who overcame great adversities and continues to do all he can to help others. He has true GRIT. Enjoy the story, then turn to Chapter 2 and begin your journey!

PASTOR UMBERTO

Tragedy can hit anyone at anytime. One minute we could be whistling a happy tune, and then the next minute we get seriously injured or hear that someone we love just died. How do you cope with tragedy? It is normal to grieve or get angry, but as the saying goes, "Life must go on." You can choose to give up, blame others, question your faith, or you can face the tragedy and move on.

Let me tell you about a man who had a terrible accident but chose to remain positive. A friend of mine traveled to Costa Rica on a mission trip. He came back with many stories, but the one that caught my attention was about Pastor Umberto. The following comes from a letter my friend sent me while on his mission trip.

While we worked we got to know some of the villagers a little better. It was fun trying to communicate with one another. Everyone was so appreciative of the fact that we had come so far just to do something that would be a blessing to them. It was very humbling. Most humbling and inspiring, however, was the testimony of Pastor Umberto. Umberto, about eight years ago, had a giant tree fall on him up in the mountains. He was pinned in a sitting position for almost four hours before a friend could return with help and enough strength to remove it. As a result, Umberto lost the use of his lower body and has been paralyzed from the waist down ever since. After going through a brief period of depression, God restored his joy and gave him a passion for life that I have never seen in another human being. For years, Umberto used a pulley and a rope (attached to a tree) to hoist himself onto his donkey so he could go and minister to other people. The village is currently raising money to buy him a Suzuki Sidekick that is equipped for someone who is disabled. As I mentioned already, Pastor Umberto is probably the happiest person I ever met. He is always smiling and often shouts out things like, "HALLELUJAH," just out of the blue.

PART TWO

GRIT: How do you get it?

CHAPTER 2
GETTING ALONG WITH OTHERS

Over a hundred years ago Theodore Roosevelt said, "The most important single ingredient in the formula of success is knowing how to get along with others." His advice is just as important today as it was back then. I like to remind my students, when they start coming up with excuses for their lack of effort or setbacks, "Remember what Roosevelt said. He said that the key to success is getting along with others. He didn't say that the key to success was, *whether you were a boy or girl, black or white, rich or poor, tall or short, high IQ or average IQ, had one parent in the home or two parents in the home.*" I also tell young people if they at least graduate from high school and have good social skills (getting along with others) they have an excellent chance for success in life.

Social skills are vital for success for everyone, young and old. My father-in-law survived a verbally abusive childhood, dropped out of school, and went off to war in the 1940's. When he returned he lost the ability to read. Even though he couldn't read **or** write he was able to operate a very successful home construction business for nearly fifty years until he died. He was able to adapt and master social skills. When he died, many people were shocked when they found he couldn't read; they didn't believe it!

How important are social skills to people today? Consider the following quotes.

"The best predictors of who will perform adequately in life include attendance, ability to stick to a task, motivation, social skills, and knowing how to prioritize and organize."
—James Comer, Child psychiatrist, Yale professor

"Repeated studies have shown that up to 85% of a child's future success depends on his or her social skills; that's more than academic achievement, economic background, family make-up, and the elusive 'who you know' factors combined."
—*The Polite Child*

"The art of dealing with people is the foremost secret of successful men. A man's success in handling people is the very yardstick by which the outcome of his whole life's work is measured."
—Paul C. Parker

"Being considerate of others will take you and your children further in life than any college or professional degree."
—Marian Wright Edleman, President & Founder of Children's Defense Fund

"There are two major things that businesses are complaining about (related to the high school graduates): tardiness and attendance. They go together into attitude and relationships. Business executives say if a kid comes in here punctually and they have a pleasant attitude, we can train them. But we can't train them if they're not on time or they're arguing with every supervisor and co-worker they come in contact with."
—Willie Judd, retired Milwaukee high school principal

"We have to emphasize communication skills, the ability to work in teams, and with people from different cultures."
—Norman Augustine, former Lockheed Martin CEO, *TIME*, December 18, 2006.

"They arrive late, talk on cell phones in class, throw temper tantrums, send ill-mannered e-mails and make threats. Sounds like a job for Super Nanny, right? Yes, if these were children. But across the nation, professors on university campuses are watching students in their classrooms sink into this abyss of rude behavior, prompting discussions on how to encourage civility without infringing on freedom of expression."

-*LA Daily News*, Oct. 21, 2006

QUIT, FIRED, SUSPENDED, DIVORCED

I'm convinced that the number one reason people can't keep a job for very long is because they can't get along with co-workers or supervisors. As a counselor I often ask my young clients why they quit their previous jobs and the most common reason/excuse they mention is their inability to get along with co-workers and/or supervisors.

School principals and teachers today will often tell you that many students have major behavior problems at school because of peer issues. Thousands of suspensions occur daily because students are arguing, teasing, bullying, and fighting each other. Their lack of social skills interferes with their learning.

The divorce rate in our country today is alarming. Years and years of research find that the top cause of divorce centers around poor communication skills. Husband and wives often have a hard time 'getting along with each other' because of their inability to sit and talk, truly listen, and share concerns. In a book I wrote several years ago, *Keeping Love Alive in the Family,* I took a list of important qualities needed in a good relationship that were devised by the late author Leo Buscaglia. I asked 300 men and women to rank the ten qualities in order of importance in a good husband/wife relationship. As I expected, communication came out #1; both women **and** men placed it at the top of their rankings. Following are the results from my survey.

- ❖ Communication—1
- ❖ Honesty—2
- ❖ Affection—3
- ❖ Compassion—4
- ❖ Romance—5
- ❖ Acceptance—6
- ❖ Dependability—7
- ❖ Sense of humor—8
- ❖ Patience—9
- ❖ Freedom—10

Good communication skills are crucial. Discipline expert Marvin Marshall reminds us, "The primary reason for communication is to reach **understanding**—not necessarily **agreement**."

Throughout the years I've collected many interesting stories of men and women dealing with marital problems; of course, most of the scenarios dealt with communication issues. Following are two of my favorites. The first tells the story of one of the most bizarre cases of a couple that just couldn't get along. After nineteen years they filed for divorce. The second tale comes from the book, *Flapdoodle, Trust & Obey*, by Virginia Cary Hudson. She shares the light-hearted story of a party invitation for a couple about to get married sometime in the 1930's or 40's.

THE BIZARRE ARIZONA DIVORCE

In 1903, Indian John Oatman married Estelle, but in 1922 Estelle filed for divorce. Did she have some valid reasons for asking the Arizona judge for a divorce from John? I'll let you be the judge. The details of this bizarre case come from the book, *Rattlesnake Blues*, by Leo Banks.

ESTELLE'S CASE AGAINST JOHN:

❖ John frightened her by putting phosphorous on his body and performing a tribal ghost dance, lighting matches to his bare feet.

❖ He strictly adhered to an ancient Mohave custom, refusing to look at his mother-in-law.

❖ He enjoyed eating locoweed and once tied her to the topmost prickly branches of a 25-foot cactus, leaving her there during a scorching hot afternoon.

❖ Estelle reported that in a gold mine explosion John lost most of his scalp, his teeth, and one of his eyes. Ever since then, Estelle complained that he delighted in removing his false teeth, popping out his glass eye, and scalping himself by removing his wig, frightening his children.

❖ She told the judge that John was having an affair with an albino Indian girl. When Estelle complained, he dug a covered pit, filled it with Gila monsters, lizards, scorpions, tarantulas, and rattlesnakes and threw her in.

❖ He played a lot poker and spent his winnings on his collection of glass eyes.

❖ One day he got angry and sawed much of the house furniture in half.

❖ He tore apart his jalopy and left all the parts on the kitchen floor.

JOHN'S SIDE OF THE STORY:

❖ He claimed that all she ever fed him was prunes and chili

con carne, prunes and tortillas, prunes and enchiladas, prunes and frijoles, and prunes and tamales.

❖ Estelle would put mud in her hair.

❖ John accused his father-in-law, George, of fraud. It seems that one day he and George were passing time in the dining room by staging a fight to death between their respective tarantulas, which met in the family sugar bowl. George had secretly sprinkled ant powder on John's tarantula, causing it to curl up and die during the battle.

The judge granted Estelle her divorce!

TEN COMMANDMENTS FOR A HAPPY MARRIAGE

The invitation for the wedding shower asked that each couple submit their "Ten Commandments for a Happy Marriage." The lists would be given to new bride and groom. Here is one of the rather interesting lists submitted by Virginia's mother.

To the bride...
1. Flatter him. Every man wants his wife to consider him an Adonis.

2. Feed him. The best way to a man's heart is still through his stomach.

3. Keep the home in order. A man's home is his castle.

4. Make him think what you want was his idea first.

5. Treat his mother as you want yours treated.

To the groom...

1. Tell her often that she is beautiful. Time will make you a convincing liar.

2. Tell her often you love her. She may always doubt you.

3. Don't begin an argument. You can't win it.

4. Don't tell her that her relatives are horrible. She knows it.

5. When all the bills are paid, divide what is left with her so she may have the little atrocities for which she longs.

The remainder of this chapter will provide readers, young and old, numerous strategies, tips, and suggestions for mastering the "G component" of the GRIT Program: getting along with others. First I'll list my thirty most important 'getting along with others' strategies. Next I'll introduce my Arenas Theory which will discuss the importance of people adapting to the many different environments/settings in which they travel through each day. Finally I list my Dozen Diffusers to help those control their anger when dealing with extremely difficult people. If more and more people mastered the "G," there would be fewer divorces, fewer students getting suspended from school, and fewer people quitting/changing jobs so often.

THIRTY 'GETTING ALONG WITH OTHERS' STRATEGIES

These thirty strategies are to be considered life-long skills; they are not "quick fix," conflict resolution skills! There are many books on the market to help you with conflict and dealing with difficult people. The strategies/skills in this book are devised to help you to, not only get along with others, but to prevent problems. Have you ever noticed there are some people who are always arguing, fussing, complaining and having serious conflicts? They seldom appear happy. Then there are those who rarely get upset and have great relationship skills with almost everybody! Why is that? Do those "happy people" know a few things that the unhappy, argumentative don't know? Medical doctor and therapist, Dr. William Glasser says, "Happy people are constantly evaluating themselves. Unhappy people are constantly evaluating others." Could it be that happier people are that way because they focus on their own actions/behaviors, things that they can control, rather than wasting their time and energy on the actions/behaviors of others? The foundation of these 'thirty' is based on the premises that you need to direct your attention to the one thing you have control over; yourself. You can't control others!

1 **It could be you!** I cannot stress this point enough. If you are having many problems getting along with others, the problem might be you! There is an old saying, "If you are always **right**, then something is **wrong**." Lately it seems that we are creating a society that wants to always blame others; it's not me, it's his fault. The evidence for this, I believe, is in the increasing use of a term I despise, *jerk*. Have you noticed how often that word is used these days? It seems that nobody thinks they are a jerk; it's always the other guy. It is amazing to me how many books are on the shelves today that are supposed to help us cope with

difficult people, and in the title of these books, the work jerk appears often. Here are a few actual book titles that you'll find in the self-help section at Barnes & Noble or Borders.

Don't Let the Jerks Get the Best of You
Jerks at Work
Joint Custody with a Jerk
Maybe he's just a Jerk
The Jerk with a Cell Phone
All Men are Jerks until Proven Otherwise
How to Work for a Jerk
Obnoxious Jerks
Make the Jerk Pay
Never Work for a Jerk
Let Me Tell You about Jerks
My Boss is a Jerk
Don't be a Jerk
How to Handle Workplace Jerks
Famous Jerks of the Bible

2 **Not everybody is going to like you and there may be some people you don't like.** This is just a fact of life. No matter how nice, kind, compassionate you are there will be a small number of people who don't like you. It may not be your fault; that's okay. Admit it; there are a few people that you have trouble liking. I wish we could eliminate the word 'hate.' I think it is alright to say, "I don't like her," but I have a problem with, "I hate her."

3 **Masterly retreats are appropriate at times.** Norman Vincent Peale once said, "Part of the happiness in life consists not in fighting battles, but in avoiding them. A masterly retreat is in itself a victory." There is nothing wrong with avoiding difficult people at times. Haven't you ever done the 'grocery store gallop'? That's when you turn down the produce aisle and see Marge and then do a quick turn down a different aisle.

4 **Understanding temperaments and personalities.** We are all born with different temperaments and personalities. Some people are easy-going and happy most of the time while others are more prone to moodiness. Learn to adapt **your** behavior when encountering people who have challenging temperaments. For instance, you may be able to give your employee Joanne some advice and she takes it well. But the same advice given to Alex sends him in to a rage.

5 **Grow some tough skin.** You can't avoid it. People will toss their hurtful "arrows" at you. The arrows are comments that could be mean, cruel, or overly-critical. Try your best not to let these arrows penetrate your skin. Pull them out and move on. Don't let Sylvia's rude morning greeting mess up the rest of your day.

6 **You can't change others!** This might be the most important thing to remember when you encounter problems with other people. You can't change others; but when you change, they change. A participant at one of my presentations told me this story to show how **our** actions can cause positive changes in others.

Three or four times a week I have to go to the counter at the post office to mail packages. It seems that most of the time I end up in Bob's line. Bob, the postmaster, isn't very friendly. He can be irritable at times, especially when I carry in several boxes to be mailed. Even though he never smiles, I still say, "Hello," and "Have a nice day." Then one day just before Christmas I got in the long line with other people getting ready to send off holiday packages. I could see that Bob was in a nastier mood than ever. I got out of line, went across the street to the coffee shop and purchased a coffee and bagel. I returned to the post office and gave the goodies to Bob and said, "You are working hard today, I hope the coffee helps." He actually smiled and said, "Thanks, I can use a coffee right now!" From that day one, Bob always greeted me with a smile, no matter how many boxes I was carrying in.

7 **Spend more time on things for which you have some control.** John Wooden, one of the greatest basketball coaches ever, says, "The more concerned we become over the things we can't control, the less we will do with the things we can control." I often remind some of the middle school girls, "What is going to help you more, spending two hours on the phone each night gossiping, talking about others, or spending two hours exercising, reading, doing some work around the house?" An article in the July, 2007 issue of *Developmental Psychology* reports on a study that found that girls who talk extensively about their problems with friends are likely to become more anxious and depressed. Researchers noted, "When girls co-ruminate, they're spending such a high percentage of their time dwelling on problems and concerns that it probably makes them feel sad and more hopeless about the problems because those problems are in the forefront of their minds. Those are symptoms of depression. In terms of anxiety, co-ruminating likely makes them feel more worried about the problems, including about their consequences. Co-rumination also may lead to depression and anxiety because it takes so much time, time that could be used to engage in other, more positive activities that could help distract youth from their problems."

8 **Spend time each day 'stacking your blocks.'** Keeping John Wooden's quote in mind, I think we all need to spend time each day doing things for ourselves. We could all benefit from exercising, reading, praying, seeking solitude, eating good food, getting enough sleep, volunteering, and enjoying hobbies. I call this 'block stacking.' Every time we do something that makes us feel good, we add a block to our stack. The taller our stack of blocks, the better we feel and the better we get along with others. If our stack of blocks is small, because we aren't finding enough "me time," the more moody, irritable, and unpleasant we become.

9 **Seek solitude.** Sometimes I think one of the best ways to get along better with others is get away from them! Seek solitude on a regular basis. While alone, think of ways you can improve personal relationships.

10 **Remember, they may be doing the best they can.** Author, Mark I. Rosen notes, "In an encounter with a difficult person, always assume, at least initially, that the person is trying to do the best he or she can and that there is a redeeming explanation for their difficult behavior." Sometimes the difficult people we meet could be struggling with family, health, or financial issues that we are not aware of. If we knew what they were going through, we would be a bit more patient, considerate, and tolerant. The following letter to *Sun* magazine (June, 2004), written by a nurse, is a perfect example of what I'm talking about.

> *I thought I was having a pretty good day at work. I knew what to do for my patients, and they seemed appreciative. My hair was behaving, I wasn't eating too much chocolate, and I was treating everyone with kindness— everyone except the new nurse. She just rubbed me the wrong way, with her sad, insecure smile. She was a little too eager, too needy. That evening I overheard the new nurse talking about her struggle to become pregnant. She'd finally had a child at the age of thirty-nine, she told the listener, but the little girl needed heart surgery, and they'd lost her to an infection. By that time, premature menopause had ended the nurse's hope for another child. Sheepishly, I asked the new nurse what the baby's name was. Her face lit up with a mother's love. "Allison. She would be five next month." She pulled out a photograph of a beautiful, bright-eyed little girl. My heart ached with shame, sadness, and awe. "Thank you," I said. What I meant was: "Thank you for teaching me how much I have to learn."*

11 **Read Hal's Dirty Thirty & Thoughtful Thirty.** One of the best books I've read on kindness, compassion, and relationships is Hal Urban's book, *Positive Words, Powerful Words*. In the book he has a list of thirty things 'not to do' and thirty things 'to do' when interacting with others. You'll have to read the book to learn all sixty, but here is a sneak preview. He surveyed hundreds of people, asking them, "What are some things you don't like to hear other people talk about?" Here are the top ten things they said they didn't want to hear: bragging, swearing and other gross-out language, gossip, angry words, lies, mean-spirited and hurtful words, judging others, playing "poor me"—the self-pity game, making discouraging remarks, embarrassing and humiliating people. Are you guilty of any of these? Let me add one more thing here about gossip. Please remember this quote, "Whoever gossips to you will gossip of you."

12 **Ask yourself, "Am I 100% sure?"** Always make sure you know all the facts before taking action, and don't believe everything you hear. Some people don't always tell the truth and/or fog the facts. Have you ever yelled at, blamed, or accused someone, only to find out later you didn't know the whole story? How did you feel? Did you apologize? I like to tell people this squirrel story as a good example of not jumping to conclusions.

TEENS TAKE THE BLAME FOR SQUIRREL'S THEFT

Davenport, Iowa: A couple has finally discovered what was happening to the yellow ribbons they were tying to the trees in their yard in support of their son and other troops in Iraq. "The ribbons started to disappear. Every time one disappeared, I would hang a new one," said Bob Saskowski, who tied the ribbons with his wife, Alexis. It went on for eight months. The last straw was when three ribbons disappeared in three days. So Bob appealed to his neighbors through a memo, asking them to talk to their teenagers about respect and patriotism and asked for their help. "It indicated I needed their eyes to help watch the trees," he said. "My husband and I were ticked," said neighbor Patty Kenyon. "And we all decided if this person was going to pick on Bob, then they can pick on all of us and we literally put yellow ribbons up and down the street." But the ribbons kept disappearing, but only from the Saskowski yard. Finally, the couple set up a video camera, focused on the yard. Six weeks later they caught the culprit on tape. The ribbon was being shimmied slowly down the trunk. At the base, the squirrel pushing the ribbon, bit through the ribbon and took off with it. "We can laugh now," Mr. Saskowski said, "Before, it was not funny." He says the squirrel was actually a good thing. "And I named him Patriot because he brought our neighborhood together."

-Kansas City Star, June 29, 2004

13 **Always be kind.** I know this isn't easy, but no matter how rude others are to you, remain kind. Returning rudeness seldom works; in fact if often makes the relationship worse. Writer Henry James said, "Three things in human life are important. The first is to be kind. The second is to be kind. The third is to be kind."

14 **Greet with a smile.** Try your best to always greet others with a smile, and if possible, say their name. "Good morning, Russell." If you are persistent and sincere, you'll eventually notice some positive changes in those people with whom you've had problems.

15 **Learn how to be an excellent listener.** Most Americans are poor listeners. Singer, songwriter Paul Williams nailed it on the head when he said, "There are those who listen, and those who wait to talk." The next time you are talking with someone, ask yourself, "Is she **really** listening to me or is she thinking about what she is going to say once I stop talking?" When someone stops by for chat, **truly** listen. Put the book down, turn away from the computer, and give him your full attention. Concentrate on his message, nod your head, and look him in the eye. When he stops talking, ask him questions, show empathy if needed, share a laugh, or acknowledge his good news. Don't change the subject until you are sure he is finished telling everything he needs to tell. Mother Teresa said, "Let no one come to you without leaving happier and better."

16 Seek out a couple of good listeners in your life. Hopefully you've got a good listener or two in your home. But for many people, there are no good listeners in their immediate family. As a counselor I've had several clients say, "Nobody listens to me!" We all need someone who listens, someone who makes us feel good to be around. One of the best listeners in my life, besides my wife, is a co-worker named John. No matter how busy he is when I stop by his office, he'll pause and say, "Hey, Tom. What's happening?" Then he remains quiet for a while and listens. Every time I leave his room, I feel better. He helps recharge my battery. No matter how much hassle you're getting from some people in your life, seek out those good listeners to help you lift your spirits. Who do you turn to you? Who truly listens to you? Who lets you vent your frustration and promises not to break confidentiality issues?

17 Get your pad and pencil. If you are having a *serious* problem coping with someone that you have frequent contact with, such as a co-worker, neighbor, relative, then you need to get *serious*! Keep this in mind; you can't change his/her behavior, but you can change yours. And, quite often, when you change, they change. When I'm having issues with someone, I'll get my pad and pencil and draw up a plan. Some people are *wing-its* and some people, like me, are *plan-its*. *Wing-its* always "go with the flow," and seldom plan ahead. Their philosophy is "whatever happens, happens." Since I'm a *plan-it*, I want a plan! I encourage you to find a quiet place, grab your pad and pencil and devise a plan of action. Write down the things you've tried that haven't worked. Ask yourself questions like: *Where are the disagreements occurring? What time of day do they happen? How do I usually respond to him/her when confronted?* Then draw up a set of new strategies to address the problem. Following is a good example of a successful plan. It is based on a true event that helped me deal with a second grade bully. Share this story with young people who may be victims of teasing or bullying.

THE "PEA-BRAIN'S" SUCCESSFUL PLAN

When I was in second grade there was a boy named Timothy who enjoyed teasing me. It all started one day when I gave a "stupid" answer to a teacher's question, and he called me a "Pea-brain." That became my nickname, and I didn't like it! Every morning he'd greet me with, "Hey Pea-brain!" After calling me the name for a few weeks, he advanced to the next level. Whenever we had peas for lunch, he would bring a few back to class. He threw them at me, put them on my seat, and once he stuck one in my ear. Timothy was sneaky; he never got caught. No matter how often I tattled on him, nothing changed. Things were getting so bad that as soon as the teacher passed out the monthly lunch menu I would look to see which days peas were on the menu. On the "pea days" I would pretend to be ill so I wouldn't have to go to school. I soon realized that since no one else was helping me, I had to solve the problem on my own, so I came up with the following plan.

A) I would stop tattling on him.

B) I would become 'invitational.' I invited him to sit with me at lunch, to be on my kickball team, and to work in my reading group.

C) I would support him and 'stick up' for him if he was being teased or bullied.

D) I would say three nice things to him every day.

E) I had to find something we both enjoyed. I found out he enjoyed collecting baseball cards, and so did I. I encouraged him to bring his cards to school. Almost every day after that, we'd sit under the playground tree trading cards. He even came to my house to play with cards.

By the end of the school year we were best of friends! I learned that changing my behavior could create positive changes in others.

18 **Always be conscious of your tone of voice.** It's been said millions of times, "It's not what you say, it's how you say it." When you are upset, take a few deep breaths and think before saying anything.

> *It's not so much what you say,*
> *as the manner in which you say it.*
> *It's not so much the language you use,*
> *as the tone in which you convey it.*
> —anonymous

19 **Let them dump the whole bucket.** If an angry person begins to vent in front of you, let him dump the whole bucket before you say anything. In other words, let him say everything he wants to say. If you interrupt him before he is finished, you may fuel his anger. Also, if someone is sharing good news, let her get it all out before asking questions or congratulating her.

20 **Don't play volleyball.** It takes at least two people to play volleyball. He hits the ball to you; you return it to him, etc. It also takes two people to argue, but seldom do arguments end well. Thomas Jefferson said, "I never saw an instance of two disputants convincing the other by argument." One of the greatest relationship skills you'll ever master is, knowing when to stop arguing and, if necessary, to excuse yourself and walk away.

21 **Learn to forgive.** Don't hold grudges or be bitter. Everyone makes mistakes, forgive them and go on with your life.

22 **Say, "I'm sorry."** Those two words are so powerful, but seldom used. According to an opinion poll commissioned by the Parker Brothers game company, Americans say, "I'm sorry" an average of only 5 times a month. Thousands of marriages could be saved every year if one of the spouses used these magic words.

23 **Keep your word.** Honesty, sincerity, trustworthiness, and keeping your word helps build positive relationships with others.

24 **Say nice things about them to others.** You may not be getting along very well with Shirley, but if you say nice things about her to others, the kind words will find their way back to her. Give it a try; you'll be surprised with the results.

25 **Acknowledge the difficulties of their jobs.** Many co-workers appear unhappy and moody. One of the reasons for this is they feel unappreciated and they don't think others realize how tough their jobs are. A quick and easy intervention for trying to develop a better relationship with these people is to simply say something like, "Chuck, you've got a tough job! I don't think others realize how many little things you do to keep things going around here! I want you to know I truly appreciate all you do. This company is lucky to have you." Parents should acknowledge how difficult school is when talking to their children.

26 Never underestimate the 'power of the pen.' Forget about emails, take out a pen, find a small card and write a nice letter to Sylvia. Make sure it is sincere. Throughout the years I've handwritten numerous notes, cards, and letters to teachers, praising them for their hard work, and I've been amazed how much the kind words meant to them. Several teachers have saved my cards and notes for many years!

27 Don't watch people, observe them. I once heard a major league baseball manager say that the most promising young players are those who, while sitting on the bench, closely observe the game, rather than just watch it. They want to learn everything they can by concentrating on the veterans players. When you observe something, you really focus on that object; you discover the smallest of details. Let's say you and Dennis, a co-worker, never seem to get along. For the next few days, observe Dennis. What kind of car does he drive? Does he drink Coke or Diet Coke? What are his hobbies? Is he married, have kids? Does he have any pets? What kind of candy bar does he purchase from the snack machine? Sneak a peek in his car and find out which CD's he is listening to these days? Where did he go to college? Is he a Democrat or Republican? Once you've done your observing, then try strategies 28 and 29.

28 Be a Trail Angel. Each year hundreds of people hike the 2,173 miles of the Appalachian Trail. Along the trail live people known as Trail Angels. They anonymously leave goodies for the hikers. They might leave fresh fruit, warm biscuits, six-packs of soda, candy, new socks, and reading material. Thanks to your observations, you know some of the things Dennis likes. When he steps away from his desk, leave a Baby Ruth. If you know he is a coin-collector, and you find an article on silver dollars, drop it on his desk. If you know he loves apples, place one in his office mailbox. Dennis may not know who the Trail Angel is, but he'll probably be in a better mood, and that may help you and him get along better.

29 **Ask him questions.** The more you know about Dennis, the more questions you can ask. Here are a few examples. *I saw you out running last night. How many miles did you run? How does your daughter like being at Boston College? How many miles a gallon does your Honda get? Great shirt! Where did you buy it? I noticed the picture of your dog. What kind of dog is it?* Simple questions like these can do so much to improve relationships. Most people love answering questions about their family, pets, and interests.

"You can make more friends in two months by
becoming more interested in other people than you can
in two years by trying to get people interested in you."
—anonymous

30 **Answer this question.** Advice expert Abigail Van Buren said, "There are two kinds of people in the world; those who walk into a room and say, "There you are!" and those you say, "Here I am!" Which one are you?

MASTERING OUR ARENAS

SNOWSHOE HARES & CHAMELEONS

Another very important element in garnering good social skills and learning how to get along better with others involves the ability to master one's arenas (settings). Throughout the day most adults travel through several different arenas. Let's use Michael for an example and follow his day. The first arena of his day is, of course, his bedroom. Then he visits the bathroom, back to his closet to dress, then to the breakfast table with his family, and he takes the dog for a walk around the neighborhood. Michael gets in his car and heads out on the freeway. When he gets to work he finds a parking place, walks in the building and greets his secretary, and sits at his desk to work at the computer. As the day goes on, he finds himself in many more arenas: lunch at the corner café, a board meeting with company officials, a stop at dentist, a quick trip to the fitness center, a meeting at the school with his daughter's teacher, choir practice at church, a trip to the family room to watch a ball game, and finally back to the bedroom to end the day. Michael has mastered these arenas; he has learned that many times a day he has to adapt/adjust his behavior. How he talks, dresses, and uses certain manners changes frequently, depending were he is and who he's with.

For the most part, adults who are happy and successful are that way because they have a good grasp on their arenas. Adults who do not have consistent control over the numerous settings in which they travel, often struggle. Because of their inappropriate behaviors in the important arenas of their lives, they are more apt to have marital problems, get in trouble with the law, and encounter problems getting and keeping jobs.

Mastering one's arenas takes a lot of hard work and experience. It isn't easy! I like to compare the human's struggles in this area with two of my favorite creatures: the chameleon and snowshoe hare. Now the chameleon has got it quite easy compared to most animals when it comes to adapting to its environments. Whenever it is threatened by an enemy, travels to a different-colored bush, or is seeking a mate, Mother Nature changes its colors automatically; the little creature doesn't have to do anything, it is automatic! Wouldn't be nice if all humans adjusted automatically and used acceptable behaviors in all settings, all the time?

Then there's the snowshoe hare. Mother Nature was not as kind to him as she was with the chameleon. Most of the year the hare has brown fur, but in winter it slowly changes to white to help it stay camouflaged in the snow. The change from brown to white can take a month or more, but when the weather plays a trick on these beautiful animals, it can be disastrous! Author and animal behavior expert, Bernd Heinrich explains the dilemma, "In the woods of western Maine the hares are almost all white by the end of November, the most usual time that there is continuous snow cover. However, in some years when the snowfall is late, the hares show up for the whole duration of lateness as if they had been marked in hunter's fluorescent orange." Because of its inability to adapt quickly on its own, it often suffers serious consequences, just like humans.

KNOCK BEFORE ENTERING: ARENA ASSISTANCE FOR ADULTS

Entering stressful arenas can be quite a challenge to many. Getting into an airplane, visiting the dentist, or getting a shot at the doctor's office can actually cause some people to become ill. Then there are those who get overly stressed every day when they enter their office at work, and there are people like me who grudgingly attend social functions with people I don't know. I believe all of us have certain arenas in our lives that we aren't excited about entering. Following are several suggestions that may help.

❖ **Positive affirmations:** Before entering the stressful setting, consider repeating a few positive affirmations such as: *This too shall pass. I'm not going to let her ruin my day. I have my health and a supportive family. I'll do my best! All days are good, but some are better than others.*

❖ **Create a personal ritual.** Take three deep breaths, snap your finger three times, look up at the beautiful sky, rub a smooth stone, or create your own ritual before entering.

❖ **Pray.** I know many people who pray, asking for guidance to help them cope. In his book, *Spiritual Notes to Myself*, Hugh Prather tells us that if we are going to pray, then we must find time to do it; no excuses! He writes:

> *If you lose your peace, break with the situation. If you need to pray, pray now. "Oh, but that might be too awkward or too much trouble," we say to ourselves. But if we had diarrhea, we would break with the situation. We would get up from the meeting. We would pull the car off the road. We would put down the phone. We would get out of line. We would excuse ourselves from the table. It's very simple: All we have to do is make the peace of God as important as diarrhea.*

❖ **Be a lioness.** Have you ever seen an animal or nature television show that describes the hunting tactics of the lioness? She is very patient and a great observer. She will wait in the bushes for hours looking at the herd of antelopes. Finally she'll target one of them and attack. I recommend the lioness tactics if you have to enter a new or uncomfortable arena. I use it! As I mentioned before, I don't like attending informal social gatherings with a lot of people I don't know. I am rather shy, but my wife is just the opposite. When she goes to these gatherings, she'll meet someone as soon as she gets in the door, a complete stranger, and strike up a long conversation. I'll be like the lioness. I will keep to myself, study the group

of people, and when I feel more at ease, I'll find someone to start up a conversation.

❖ **Keep a can of 'suck it up' close by.** Sometimes we just
have to devour a can of 'suck it up.' Deal with it, get
over it, and move on! I have a can of it when I go to the
dentist office.

❖ **6 'don'ts' when dealing with a difficult person in an
arena.** Whether it's at a party, church, work, school, or
in the neighborhood, we all, at one time or another, will
encounter difficult people. Psychotherapist, Bill
Borcherdt, in the book *Think Straight, Feel Great!*, suggests these 'don'ts' when confronted:

—Don't deny the allegation or the other's account of your
shortcomings.

—Don't get defensive and think you have to spell out and
prove your goodness and the badness of what was
spewed your way.

—Don't counterattack by aggressively bad mouthing your
attacker.

—Don't over-explain or make any effort to convince your
tormenter of something he or she doesn't want to be convinced of.

—Don't apologize for something that may not have been
your fault or responsibility to begin with.

—Don't justify yourself and your existence in a humble,
atoning way.

❖ **When all else fails.** If your arena-struggles begin to take
a toll on your health, job, or family, you might want to
consider these options.

—Seek professional help.

—Discuss concerns with your pastor or a friend you trust.

—Read. Our libraries and book stores are over-flowing with excellent publications on all kinds of topics. I suggest reading biographies of people who overcame personal struggles.

—Many people today are hiring personal coaches for guidance.

SPITTING, BURPING, & NODDING

As I travel the country doing workshops, I discover subtle differences in language, customs, rituals, and traditions. Even though I enter new arenas, I seldom have to make major adjustments because throughout the United States many of the rules, laws and manners are about the same. But, traveling to a different country can be quite challenging if I don't prepare. Certain behaviors that are acceptable in the United States may be considered rude in another country and vice versa. Here are three examples I like to share with others.

❖ In the late 1890's, Colonel J.H. Patterson traveled from England to Africa to build new railroads. In one of his first visits with the Masai tribe, he was introduced to its leader. Patterson held out his hand in a friendly gesture, but the Masai ruler spit on him. No one told Patterson about the tribe's unique way of greeting visitors.

❖ Burping at the dinner table is a sign of poor manners in our country, but when the Bengali people do it, it is a sign of appreciation; the food was good!

❖ If you want to signal 'no' in Albania, nod. If you want to say 'yes,' shake your head. This is very important to know if you plan to go there!

ARENA ASSISTANCE FOR YOUNG PEOPLE

The Boy on the Track

One evening I was doing some speed-work on the university's track. Midway through my workout I noticed a boy (about 12 years-old) walking laps. I'm always pleased to see young people exercising. The boy stayed on the inside lane and walked slowly as fast runners lapped him. After a lap or two I could see he was getting frustrated; he had a puzzled look on his face. I soon discovered why. When serious runners are doing speed-work on a track, they demand the inside lane. When the runners whizzed by the boy they fussed at him. When they approached him they shouted "track." In running lingo this means move out of the inside lane, a faster runner is coming. The more they shouted and fussed, the sadder he got. I didn't want this young runner to get discouraged and quit exercising so I called him over to the edge of the track and explained to him proper track etiquette. I told him why the fast runners were shouting "track." He smiled and said, "Thank you; I didn't know why they were mad at me. Now I'll move out of the way when then come by." Off he went! As he left I realized that no one had ever explained to him how to behave in this arena. I also thought, "This is another perfect example of how many young people's behavior appears to be rude or inappropriate, when the reason why, is that a lot of adults are guilty of not teaching kids how to behave in the many arenas they visit each day." It's not always the children's fault! They need to be educated.

Adolescent Arenas

Most elementary-aged children are receptive to our arena lessons; they want to please us. But working with adolescents is a much bigger challenge because they often have two sets of behaviors: 1) How they act around adults, 2) How they act around their peers. This is a big dilemma for them. We need to be cognizant of the peer-related issues our middle and high school-aged children are going through. Our young people categorize each other into groups or cliques such as the *jocks, preppies, nerds, druggies, skateboarders, losers, gothics,* and others. Then there are the pressures to get involved in smoking, drinking, drugs, and risk-taking actions. Bullying and teasing can occur based on looks, clothing, and possessions (who has a cell phone, laptop computer, iPod, and who doesn't). Parents need to do their best they can to have their children to do the right thing, but even the good kids will slip off the track once in a while. I also discourage parents from saying, "My kid would never do that!" Can you remember a few bad things you did when you were young that your parents never knew about it?

16 TIPS FOR HELPING KIDS MASTER THEIR ARENAS

1 **Modeling.** The best strategy for helping our children master their arenas is proper modeling by adults. They are always watching us. If you don't want your children to use profanity, then you shouldn't. How do you handle conflicts on the highway? Do you yell, flip the middle finger, or shout out obscenities? Are you quiet during the moment of silence at the ballpark? Do you model good manners at the dinner table? How do you handle conflicts with your spouse when the children are watching?

2 **Be consistent.** If you have a rule about 'no hats at the dinner table,' stick to it every day. Don't address the issue one day and then ignore it the next. The more consistent you are, the more likely children will comply.

3 **Utilize the Kindergarten Rule.** Have you visited a kindergarten classroom lately? If you have, you'll notice that almost every time the students get ready to leave the room, the teacher will review rules and expectations. "Now, boys and girls, after you wash your hands, line up quickly. Remember, be quiet in the halls and keep your hands to yourself. In the cafeteria make sure you get at least one fruit and vegetable, and be sure to say 'thank you' to the ladies." Make it a habit to remind your children, even adolescents, about rules, procedures, and your expectations as they visit different settings.

4 **Gradually expose them to various arenas when they are young.** As they mature, take them to restaurants, zoos, museums, libraries, and church. As much as possible, do it as a family. For instance, if you have a strong faith and you believe everyone in the family needs to go to church, then take the children when they are little, do it every Sunday, then they often get to expect it; it's a family ritual. But don't expect fifteen year-old Jimmy, who's never been to church, to be excited about your invitation.

5 **Don't bribe or reward them.** Good behavior is to be expected! It's required! Avoid saying, "I'll give you a candy bar if you behave in the grocery store." Will Lucy behave to get the candy bar, **or** will she behave because it is the right thing to do? It is okay to celebrate progress. For example, you notice that Lucy has improved her grocery store behavior lately. Then the next day when she comes home from school you say, "Lucy, let's celebrate your progress. You've been doing so much better at the grocery store. Where do you want to go tonight for dinner?"

6 **Acknowledge more, praise less.** Earlier in this book I talked about our generation of "praise junkies." Hopefully one of your goals is to have your children behave appropriately wherever they go. Children need to behave, as mentioned in #5, because it is the right thing to do, not because they are seeking praise and goodies. A little praise is deserved occasionally, but try this strategy more often. Acknowledge instead of praise. Here is an example. Instead of saying, "Missy, I'm so proud of you for opening the door for Mrs. Jones," say, "Missy, I saw you open the door for Mrs. Jones." You've let her know that you saw her good deed and often that will suffice.

7 **Tell them to do the right thing.** Whenever your child leaves the house, say "I love you" and "Do the right thing!" Does your child know the right thing to do?

8 **Be aware of the conduct of your child's coaches and youth group leaders.** Are their behaviors acceptable and closely related to your philosophy of working with children? I know there are many middle and high school football coaches who use a lot of profanity, and then there are those who never use any. Does that matter to you?

9 **Non-negotiables.** In each arena, especially homes and schools, there need to be a few rules. Some rules may be a bit vague and misinterpreted at times, but both arenas must have a small number of specific rules that are clear cut, easy to understand, and are not open to discussion. These may include such things as: no hitting, no profanity, no taking things from others without asking, and no leaving without permission.

10 **Accept but don't approve.** Your children must know your value system. They should know where you stand on important issues such as smoking, drinking, fighting, bullying, teasing, music lyrics, and violence. Let's take music for example. You hear one of the songs on your teenage son's newest CD's and it contains lyrics that degrade women. You need to say something; don't ignore it. By ignoring, it lets your son think it is okay. Reply, "I don't approve of those lyrics. I don't want to hear it in my car or living room. Degrading women is wrong! If you are going to listen to it, do it in your room." Sure, it would seem easier to just say, "I don't ever want to hear you listening to that CD again!" But, he will find another time and place to listen to it. Here's another example. If you don't like pierced ears on men and your eighteen year-old son comes one with his ears pierced, you could say, "I don't approve of it, but I'll accept it."

11 **Give children 'some' control over their bedroom arena.** When your child enters adolescence, consider giving her more control over her bedroom. Let her paint it her favorite color, don't get overly concerned if it gets too cluttered, give her input into curtains, and furnishings. Sometimes all parents have to decide which battles to fight and which ones to ignore. With my own children, I chose not to fight the bedroom battle.

12 **Don't ignore environmental issues.** The most important arena out there is the earth. Teach children the importance of recycling, being kind to animals, not wasting natural resources, not littering, and how to avoid polluting our air and water.

13 **Give each child a can of 'suck it up.'** At an early age remind your children that 'life isn't always fair.' They'll encounter mean teachers, bad umpires, cheaters, and rude people. We need to do all we can to encourage our children to resolve problems on their own. So the next time Henrietta says, "That wasn't fair," or Bucky pleads, "The umpire is blind," reply, "Here's a can of 'suck it up.' Now get over it and move on!"

14 **Look for teachable moments.** If you are walking down the street with your eight year-old, and you both witness someone littering, take advantage of the event to teach a lesson. "Billy, it is wrong to do what he did. It's against the law plus it makes the streets look dirty."

15 **Try these four arena interventions when they don't comply.** When your child is not behaving appropriately, such as running in Wal-Mart (of course you already explained to him your store behavior expectations, didn't you?) try this step-by-step plan.

a) Use the word 'what.' *Lindy, what are you doing? What rule are you breaking? What could happen if you fall? What are you going to do instead of running?* Don't say, "Why are you running?" Dumb question! I'll explain this more in the next chapter.

b) If he continues, take him aside. Be sterner and state a consequence that you can follow through with when you get home (i.e. to bed early, no television tonight, or 15 minutes timeout).

c) If he continues, then follow through with stated consequence.

d) If his store behavior doesn't improve then he loses that privilege for a period of time. Missing the next trip to the store may be a wake-up call!

16 **Extracurricular activities are a must.** Children need to spend time other places than home and school. In order to master social skills, meet new friends, and build on athletic and artistic abilities, parents are encouraged to get their children involved in such things as sports, scouts, church, band, martial arts, dance, gymnastics, and after-school clubs. Elementary children should participate in at least two of these on a yearly basis. Middle school and high school students are recommended to participate in a minimum of three. Closely monitor teenager's involvement. Don't let them get involved in too many activities; their academics and family life may suffer. They'll burn themselves out! My research finds that children who keep busy in positive after-school activities tend to stay out of trouble, graduate, and become important members of society.

Danny's Dilemma

As a professional counselor I work with people of all ages who need assistance adapting to challenging arenas. The following is a story about an eighth grade boy, Danny (not his real name) who I assisted. I'll break down my strategies/recommendations in a simple step-by-step outline that might help you or someone else who has a similar problem. Danny was referred to me by his parents because he was having issues with his math teacher. His parents noted that he was skipping class, his grades were dropping, and twice, the math teacher sent him to the principal for being disrespectful. He visited me in October, which meant he had several more months to go in that class.

1) **Listen.** I let him tell me his story. I truly listened. I used good eye contact and nodded often. I remained quiet as much as possible as I let him 'dump the whole bucket.' I didn't interrupt or ask questions, except for simple clarification. As I listened to him, I realized I was hearing his side of the story. I'm sure if I talked to his teacher I might get a different slant.

2) Empathize. When he finished I acknowledged his frustration, but I didn't dwell on it. I made a couple short comments. *I can tell you are frustrated. I'm sorry things aren't going well. School can be tough at times.*

3) Value statement. I asked, "Do you like the way things are going?" Then, "Are you ready to seriously address the problem?"

4) Tom's #1 relationship fact. I tell him my most important rule, "You can't change others; you can only change yourself. But when you change, they change."

5) Strategies. Once I got him to understand that he couldn't withdraw from that math class (he needed it to go on to high school) and that he couldn't change the teacher's "attitude problem" (that's what Danny called it), then he needed to try the following strategies.

—Get to class on time with completed homework.

—Always greet the teacher.

—Respond to the teacher with, "Yes, sir."

—Participate in class.

—Get to know the teacher better. Is he married? Have pets? What are his hobbies? Once you know more about him, ask him questions about those things. *Did you watch that game last night? How's Sparky doing these days? Did you read that article in the newspaper last night about the famines in Africa?*

—While in his class, don't associate with other misbehaving students.

—Compliment/thank him. *That was a great lesson. Thanks for the help.*

6) Feedback. After Daniel implemented these strategies, we reviewed. My goal was to get him to realize that he needed to be proactive and that when he changed his behavior, there was a good chance that his teacher's behavior would change.

A DOZEN DIFFUSERS*

I believe that anger is an excellent "friend repellent." People are hesitant to get close to those who are easily angered. As I finish this chapter on getting along with others I offer twelve quick strategies to help young and old get better control of the most dangerous emotion of all. Once anger is under control, friends return, marital relations improve, and there will be fewer problems with co-workers.

1 **Sit down.** Anger decreases when you sit; it increases when you stand. If you have a conflict with someone, take advice from this Native American saying, "Standing is confrontation, sitting is conversation."

2 **Look up!** Don't look at the person who is fueling your anger. Look up at the ceiling or the sky for at least ten seconds. Believe it or not, your anger loosens its grip.

3 **Inhale some pleasant fragrances.** Keep some liquid soap or hand lotion close by. Rub the lotion on your hands. The movement of your hands will burn off the extra energy, plus the pleasing odor is calming. The best fragrances are lavender, peach, strawberry, and wintergreen.

4 **Practice 'square breathing.'** A square has four sides. Square breathing involves four steps. 1) Breathe in slowly for four seconds, 2) Hold your breath in for four seconds, 3) Take four seconds to let the air out, 4) Pause for four more seconds before doing or saying anything.

5 **Chew sugarless gum.** Keep a pack in your purse or pocket. Have a piece and chew your anger away.

6 **Look in the mirror.** When you are angry, the only one who doesn't see your "not so pretty face" is you! Find a mirror and take a close look. That should help you simmer.

7 **Count colors.** Angry people are often told to count to ten, but psychologist Leonard Felder recommends counting colors (at least twelve different ones). He believes this works because it activates the areas of the brain that usually shut down when one becomes angry.

8 **A cup of chamomile please.** Drink a cup of chamomile tea. This herbal tea is known for its ability to help people stay calm and relaxed.

9 **Go west by sailing east.** If you live in Georgia and want to go to California, you would travel west, but can you get to California by going east? Yes, but it will take longer. When you get upset with someone, don't take the shortest route towards him; take the long way. Walk around the room, go outside, get a drink of water and then you'll have time to calm down before talking to him.

10 **Do the grizzly bear growl.** I use this one often. Instead of screaming, pretend you are a grizzly bear, get up on your toes, stick your paws & claws up high and growl loudly for several seconds. Not only does the anger leave, but peacefulness overcomes you.

11 **Practice thought-stopping.** This is a quick, simple, no nonsense tactic. As soon as you feel anger approaching, tell yourself, "Stop!"

12 **Use the pressure-point.** Take your thumb and press it firmly to the tip of your middle finger for ten seconds. This helps burn off energy and it delays your response/reaction.

*These strategies were adapted from my two books that are published by YouthLight, Inc.
- *131 Creative Strategies for Reaching Children with Anger Problems*
- *141 Creative Strategies for Reaching Adolescents with Anger Problems*

CHAPTER 3
RESPONSIBILITY

PUSRSUING HAPPINESS

I truly believe that everyone wants to be happy; but not everyone accomplishes that goal. What is the secret? Why do some find happiness, while others never do? I think the key to being happy starts with being responsible. I plan to use the following three quotes as a starting point in this chapter to lead adults and children on their way to becoming more cheerful.

"Happy people are responsible people.
Responsible people are happy people."
—Marvin Marshall

"Your joy is your responsibility."
—Joyce Meyer

"The. U.S. Constitution doesn't guarantee happiness, only the pursuit of it. You have to catch up with it yourself."
—Benjamin Franklin

Marvin Marshall's quote

I love his quote! It is few in words, but it makes so much sense to me. Let's examine it. He claims that happy people are responsible. It's true most of the time. Think about. Adults who have good health, eat well, exercise on a regular basis, find time for their spiritual enrichment, spend quality time with family members, enjoy and are effective in their jobs, give back to their communities, are constantly learning, have several hobbies/interests, keep finances under control, and find time for themselves tend to be content, joyful. And, of course, just the opposite is true; adults who do not keep up with some of these positive behaviors lean toward unhappiness. It is a tough balancing act at times, especially when tragedy hits. Serious illness, death of a loved-one, job lay-offs, divorce, or major financial problems can test even the happiest of us!

Children's happiness is also related to being responsible. I tell my students, "If you do your chores, do your homework, take care of your belongings, be respectful, follow rules at home and school, you seldom get fussed at, and when you don't get fussed at, you tend to be happy. Don't keep up with your responsibilities at school and home, you'll get fussed at, punished, and privileges taken away, then you won't be a happy camper!" Several teachers at my school have posters on their walls that read, "Responsible kids are happy kids." When their students don't complete their work or they misbehave, the teachers will say, "Are you being responsible?"

Joyce Meyer's quote

Joyce Meyer is a popular evangelist and Christian book author. I enjoy watching her weekly television show. More than once I've heard her say, "Joy is your responsibility." If you sit back and expect joy to come to you, good luck! Yes, some joy may come your way if you sit and wait, but if you desire much joy, you need to go get it! History tells us that many of the wealthiest kings and queens, those who had all kinds of gifts laid at their feet, were not cheerful. We need to get off our 'thrones' and take more responsibility for our well-being.

Are our children full of joy? It may appear that way at times, but take a close look at this common occurrence. It's Saturday morning. Mom looks in the living room where her two children are sitting on the floor, eating Fruit-loops, and laughing at cartoons. Oh, they look so happy. Later the kids head to the video games and computers. She hears them giggling. For lunch the kids cheer as mom says, "Let's go to Burger King!" Later that day, the kids are watching movies, eating potato chips, and drinking soda. They never go outside to play and there are no chores! Before bed it's more television and junk food. Mom is so happy because her kids had a fun day. Let's hope this isn't a typical day. If it is, look out! They may appear happy now, but later in life they could face poor health from lack of exercise, obesity, diabetes, poor social skills, and, because they had no chores and other family responsibilities growing up, they may have trouble running their own households.

Benjamin Franklin's quote

He stresses the importance of pursing happiness. It's out there, but we have to find it; it won't come looking for us. This chapter will provide readers with practical ideas to help in the search. I've divided the 'pursuit' into two areas:

> *The inner-self:* I'll focus on things that we have much control over, especially in the areas of our physical, emotional, and spiritual well-being. We do have control over what we eat, our fitness, learning, spirituality, and attitude. It is our responsibility to take care of our mind and body.

> *The outer-self:* There are many things that happen in our lives that we don't have total control of.

> We don't have total control over other people's behavior, including our spouse and children. We don't have a lot of input into issues of terrorism, racism, pollution, global warming, the homeless and crime, but I strongly feel that it is our responsibility to address these issues. It is our responsibility to do all we can to make our communities and the world better places in which to live and be happier.

Before we begin the search, enjoy the following tale of two men's unique journeys to find happiness. There are many versions of this story, but this one is adapted from Richard Mahler's book, *Stillness: Daily Gifts of Solitude*.

CONTENTMENT IN A SLEEPY MEXICAN COASTAL VILLAGE

A wealthy middle-aged investment banker from New York took a vacation in a small coastal Mexican village. As he walked along the water he noticed a lone fisherman in a small boat haul in a large catch. The fisherman, who appeared to be about the same age as the banker, brought in a couple more tuna.

"How long did it take you to catch them?" asked the vacationer.

"Just a few minutes," the Mexican replied.

As the fisherman paddled in, the banker asked him why he didn't stay out longer and catch more fish. He responded, "I take just enough to support me and my family."

"What do you do the rest of the day?"

"I sleep late in the morning before I go fishing. When I return I play with my kids, take a *siesta* with my wife, maybe go fishing again, eat dinner, then stroll the plaza with my *amigos*. We have a few drinks, sing, and play guitar. I keep busy and enjoy life."

The banker scratched his head, thought for a minute, then told the man, "I have an MBA from Harvard and I think I can give you some ideas so you could buy a bigger boat and catch even more fish. Once you start increasing your catch you could sell even more to the processor and eventually earn enough money to open your own cannery. That would give you control over product, processing, and distribution. You'd make so much money you could leave this little village and buy a huge mansion near Mexico City and open your own business headquarters."

The fisherman gave the New Yorker a puzzled look and asked, "How long would that take?"

"About twenty years."

"And then what?" asked the fisherman.

The banker chuckled, "That's the best part. When the timing is right, you sell your business, and you'll be rich!"

The Mexican grinned, "*Si, senor,* and after I retire I could move to a sleepy coastal village where I could sleep late, fish, play with my kids, fish some more, take *siestas* with my wife, and after dinner head the plaza to join my friends."

THE INNER-SELF

IT TAKES GRIT TO BE FIT!

Let's talk about the body first. God only gave us one, and it is our responsibility to take care of this precious gift. It isn't always easy! Yes, you'll need a lot of grit! Over the years I have struggled in this area. When I graduated from high school I weighed 165 pounds, and at one time in my life I *blossomed* to 237! Controlling my weight, thanks to some of the 'not-so-good' genes I inherited, will always be an issue for me. I've been able to gain much control by getting "addicted" to running and changing eating habits.

What enters our mouths is our decision. As adults, we can smoke, abuse alcohol and drugs, skip breakfast, and load up on junk food if we wish. Even though many adults are guilty of such habits, they are cognizant of the negative consequences. Almost everyone who smokes or is overweight realizes that he or she needs to make some changes.

When we talk about weight-control, good nutrition, and exercise, almost every one of us knows what we need to do to address these issues. Ask anyone how to lose weight and he will probably say, "Eat food with less calories and exercise." Duh! Do we not know that? Do we, as a nation, need to invest billions of dollars every year on diet books to tell us these things? Thousands of studies reveal to us that over 90% of people who follow some of the numerous fad diets mentioned in the latest books, do lose weight for a while, but eventually gain the weight back. I belong to a book club that mails me a monthly listing of various publications. Every month they list a bunch of diet books. Here are a few that were in the July, 2007 mailing:

THE SONOMA DIET COOKBOOK

THE TOP 100 DIET SECRETS

THE F-FACTOR DIET

THE pH MIRACLE for WEIGHT LOSS

THE SIMPLE PLAN: ULTRA METABOLISM

ATKINS for LIFE

WEIGHT WATCHERS NEW COOKBOOK

YOU on a DIET

THE SELF-HYPNOSIS DIET

RETHINKING SLIM

Book publishers are always looking for clever diet books. Why? Because they sell! Publishers aren't looking for practical, common sense books on how to lose weight. The following letter to *Sun* magazine helps prove my point.

> *As an official "EXPERT ON WEIGHT MAN-AGEMENT," I've been helping people lose weight since 1977. In that time, there's one thing I've learned; it is much easier to lose weight than keep it off. Anyone who claims otherwise is either naïve or a scoundrel. Of the multitude of dieting programs that make up the $30 billion weight-loss industry, remarkably few follow up to find out what happened to the people who invested their faith, time, energy, and money in the product. According to the weight-loss programs that do keep follow-up data, most participants regain the weight after six months or a year. By five years, more than 90 percent have gained it all back. Several years ago, a colleague and I wrote a book about some of those rare people who have lost fifty pounds or more and kept it off for at least five years. These amazing individuals had one thing in common:*

*each had found his or her own way—no diet, book, pro-
gram, or person was the 'Answer.' What these people did
was never quick or easy. They followed trails of clues,
trusted intuition, and confronted truths about themselves
and their world that they had not wanted to see. A single
mother of six saved enough money to hire a sitter for an
hour once a week so she could ride her bike. Another
woman, recognizing her loneliness, divorced her gay
husband, brought up her three children alone, and
joined a quilting group for fellowship. One man joined a
twelve-step program and started meditating. Not sur-
prisingly, thirteen publishers rejected the book. All
asked that we write a diet book instead.*

G.N. –Portland, OR

Please forgive me if I appear a bit cynical here. I am aware
that there are a small number of people with certain health
issues that aren't their fault, and that weight control is extremely difficult, but most people have no excuses for not make
changes. Some diet books do offer great ideas, but keep a few
things in mind while reading them. Ask yourself, "Is this diet a
fad, quick fix, or something that I can stick with that will help
me make positive **life-long** changes?" Also, ask yourself if the
book recognizes the importance of exercise.

GOOD NUTRITION: MAKING
POSITIVE LIFE-LONG CHANGES

*The average American consumes in a 72-year lifetime
approximately eleven cattle, three lambs, three sheep, 23 pigs,
45 turkeys, 1,100 chickens and 862 pounds of fish.*
—Hinduism Today, Jan. 2007

*The Worldwatch Institution reports that the per-capita
American sugar consumption today (2005) is 2.5 times what it
was in 1961, with Americans consuming an average of 686*

calories of sugar per day. That equals three candy bars per American daily, and a third of the recommended 2,200 calorie daily intake for the typical person snarfed as sugar alone.
—Gregg Easterbrook, The Progress Paradox

They call this a Happy Meal? With all the fat, sugar, and calories in it, they should call it an Unhappy Meal!
—overheard at a fast-food restaurant

There are at least three important reasons for taking more responsibility for maintaining a healthy diet: 1) You will be healthier, look better, have more energy, and feel better, 2) You do it for your family members because you increase the odds that you'll live longer and 'always be there' for them, 3) You are modeling good nutrition for your children.

Healthy eating is not that complicated. You don't need to purchase one of those $30 diet books! Try following my list of "Nutrition Nuggets."

NINE NUTRITION NUGGETS

1 Use the green, yellow, red food color system for yourself and your children. Relate the color code system to a traffic light. **Green** foods include most vegetables and fruits. You can eat all you want. **Yellow** foods are meant to be eaten in moderation. They include whole wheat breads, pasta, dairy products, beans, and nuts. **Red** foods must be avoided as often as possible: sugars, candy, cookies, cakes, high-calorie sodas, saturated fats. Don't ever forget that you are the adult/parent. You control which food items find their way into your cupboards and refrigerator!

2 Implement the 80/20 Theory. Eighty percent of the time eat "good" food. This allows you to slip off the track once in a while to treat yourself to a favorite sweet snack.

3 Drink a lot of water.

4 Eat a good breakfast, something that will stick with you until lunch; oatmeal, All-Bran cereal, Grape Nuts, whole wheat toast with peanut butter, and fruit.

5 Write down everything you eat. Yes, keep a calorie log. Determine how many calories a day you should consume in order to lose weight, and then determine how many calories to maintain your weight. For instance, I try to eat between 2,500-2,800 calories a day. When I finally adjusted to that level, my body adapted. It got use to that amount. If I eat less, my body fusses at me; if I eat more, I feel bloated, yucky. When training for a marathon I up the calories a bit.

6 Pack your lunch. Take a few minutes every morning to pack a healthy lunch. It's cheaper than going to a restaurant, and it ensures that you'll get a more nutritious, lower calorie meal. Once you get in the habit of packing your lunch, you rarely have the desire to order take-out. Monday through Friday I bring the same items to work in my brown bag: water, a bag of peanuts, a peanut butter/jelly sandwich, and two apples. My co-workers wonder how I can eat the same thing every day; I can't imagine eating anything else. If I don't get my peanut butter/jelly sandwich, I go bonkers!

7 Get involved with your child's school. Does the school have a nutrition policy? Do they follow it? Do teachers allow students to keep water bottles on their desks? Are teachers using candy as a reinforcer? Are there vending machines available to students that are filled with soda, sugary fruit drinks, and potato chips? Do the adults at school model good nutrition? Now days, if I still had school-age children, I'd pack their lunches!

8 Be a grazer. As I mentioned earlier in this book, I am an observer of people. I've noticed that many active, thin people are grazers. And, their snacks are usually healthy. Instead of eating three big meals a day, consider eating six-eight smaller meals.

9 Get active! Eating well is only half of the formula for good health. Adults need at least thirty minutes a day, five days a week, of **vigorous** exercise. Did you notice I highlighted the word vigorous? You **must** get that heart rate up! Also, are you encouraging your children to be active? Does your child's school emphasize the importance of physical fitness?

FIND TIME FOR EXERCISE; NO EXCUSES!

You want to look better, feel better, and have more energy? Get the body moving and get that heart rate up! Just as you have control over what you eat, you do have much control over your physical fitness. Here are a few tips to get you going.

No excuses! You must make exercise a priority. There are 168 hours in the week; can you find two or three hours for your heart? Remember, you are modeling for your children. If you keep coming up with excuses, they will to.

Select an activity. Explore your options: brisk walking, running, swimming, biking, treadmill, martial arts, aerobics, dance, and other vigorous activities. Try your best to find one that you enjoy. I believe the minimum time to spend on your activity is thirty minutes a day, five days a week. Hopefully you'll be able to increase your exercise time even more as you get in better shape.

Be patient. Sometimes it will take a month or two to get hooked. Most people quit their new exercise programs after a few days; make a vow to yourself to stick with it for at least four weeks. After that, it often becomes a habit. Author and medical doctor, William Glasser, wrote a fascinating book, *Positive Addiction*. In the book he tells how people can actually become addicted to their physical activities. For instance, if you swim every day for several months, and then stop, you could actually suffer withdrawal symptoms such as sluggishness, mood swings, and inability to sit and focus. I consider running as my addiction. If I go two days in a row without hitting the road, I'm not an easy guy to live with; just ask my wife!

Don't feel guilty. Many parents feel guilty when they 'abandon' their families to go out walking, running, or biking. Don't! You deserve your time alone. Also, by getting fit you'll find yourself being a better parent and spouse. You'll be more relaxed, less-stressed, and easier to get a long with!

Get creative. In our busy world, sometimes it is hard to find time to do our physical activities. You'll have to get creative. Can you get up earlier in the morning? Can you do it at lunch time? Can you and your spouse take turns watching the kids so each of you has your time? Can you and your neighbor share babysitting duties, allowing more flex time? How about a baby jogging stroller? I remember when I started running. On the days my wife went to work I would put my two children in their playpen and placed it in the middle of the back yard. Then I would jog the perimeter of the property, while keeping an eye on the kids.

Don't forget the kids. Encourage, invite, but don't force your children to get active. Forcing seldom works. The best way to get your children active is to have them witness you being active. At my school I've noticed that a high percentage of our physically fit kids have parents who are fit. Every one of us needs to do all we can to get young people active. Almost daily I read articles about our young people becoming more and more overweight, and for many, obese. A good number of these kids are targets for diabetes as they get older. In the July 13, 2007 issue of *USA WEEKEND*, Dr. Ted Mitchell wrote:

A non-drug treatment has been shown not only to help those with diabetes but also to prevent those at risk from developing it. That treatment is exercise. For years, studies have shown that physical activity enhances a cell's uptake of glucose, getting the sugar to where it's needed for the cell to function normally. When it comes to treating diabetes, it's difficult to overstate how important it is to remain physically active.

One final note on exercise; don't let age be a factor. No matter your age, you can still keep active. Read this about one remarkable senior citizen.

Suzie on the Run

I travel throughout the state of North Carolina participating in road races ranging from 5K's to marathons. Several times I noticed a married couple at many of the races, traveling with their dogs. The wife was the runner; he was the coach. Prior to each race he would help her stretch, massage her legs and back, and provide her with words of encouragement. Then he and the dogs would head to the starting line to watch her take off. At one of the races I struck up a conversation. He told how his wife, Suzie Kluttz, couldn't wait until next year when she would turn seventy years-old. Yes, she was excited about turning seventy because that would put her in a new age-group (70-74) at races and she felt she could break the national record for women in the 5K (3.1 miles). A few months later I picked up my *Running Journal*, and read, "Suzie Kluttz set a pending 5K national record for 70-74 women at the Morganton race, covering the course in 24:23." Wow!

Get outside.

The average American spends 96% of the time indoors. Many highway commuters in big cities spend more time in their cars than they do outside. A hundred years ago, Americans got outside and walked an average of three miles per day, and today average a quarter-mile. I laugh when I hear people complain about the weather when they are rarely in it! For some people the only time they go outside is to get in and out of their cars. We are becoming an indoor society and that concerns me. There is a Native American saying, "The more we remove ourselves from the land, the worse our behavior gets." It's bad enough that adults don't get outside, but children aren't outside. When I'm out running or driving my car, it astonishes me how few children I see outdoors.

I encourage you to spend more time in the sun. Consider taking part of your exercise program outside. Breathe in the morning air, hear the birds, study the clouds, and appreciate our beautiful planet. Anne Frank provides us with more reasons for getting outside, "The best remedy for those who are afraid, lonely, or unhappy is to go outside, somewhere where they can be quite alone with the heavens, nature and God. Because only then does one feel that all is as it should be and that God wishes to see people happy, amidst the simple beauty of nature."

Now, let's talk more about children getting outdoors. First of all, think how the terms 'in' and 'out' have changed during the last twenty or thirty years. Back in the 1960's when I was a kid and I went to visit my best friend Donnie and asked his mother where he was, she always prefaced his whereabouts with the word, 'out.' She would say that Donnie was: out riding his bike, out hunting, out fishing, out playing baseball, out mowing the yard, out playing with the dog, etc. Now days when a child asks where his friend is, the mother will preface his whereabouts with the word, 'in.' She'll say he is: in his room, in on the phone, in on the computer, in playing video games, etc. One way to help our children acquire grit is to encourage them to get outside in the elements; playing in the sun, running in the rain, building a snowman, playing baseball or shooting hoops on a cold afternoon, riding bikes in the cool evening air or catching fireflies in the dark.

While most would agree children need to be outdoors more often, there appears to be an "outdoors is dangerous" myth in our country. "Oh, little Johnny might fall out of the tree or Condie might get kidnapped, or Hank could get a tick in his hair." In fact, Conn and Hal Iggulden have written a neat book, *The Dangerous Book for Boys*. The authors encourage children to get outside, build forts, make go-carts, make bows and arrows, tie knots, and other 'risky' behaviors like kids did years ago. In the first chapter they list the essential gear that boys should carry with them: Swiss army knife, compass, handkerchief, box of matches, a shooter (marble), needle and thread, pencil and paper, small flashlight, magnifying glass, band-aids, and fishhooks. Boys caught carrying these items around today might be called junior-terrorists! Imagine what would happen to these boys if they brought some of these items to school!

I've been doing a lot of research on this topic, hoping to dispel the myth that being outdoors is dangerous for children. The only place the outdoors is dangerous is in a high crime area, infested with drug dealers and gangs. I've read numerous research articles on kidnappings, abductions, and abuse. I've also read several excellent books that examine children's safety. Much of the information on my list that follows comes from these two books: *Last Child in the Woods: Saving our Children from Nature Deficit Disorder*, by Richard Louv and *Paranoid Parenting*, by Frank Furedi.

REASONS WHY CHILDREN ARE SAFER & HEALTHIER OUTSIDE THAN INSIDE

1   **The air is often healthier outside.** Many homes are filled with dusty, dirty air. *The Journal of Allergy and Clinical Immunology*, reported in 2005, "More than half of all Americans test positive in response to one or more allergies, double the percentage who did 30 years ago." One theory why,

according to the researchers, is that people simply don't go outside as often and have higher exposures to indoor allergies. According to Richard Louv, "Indoor air pollution is the nation's number-one environmental threat to health—and it's two to ten times worse than outdoor air pollution, according to the Environmental Protection Agency."

2 **Children are exposed to more violence in the home.** They spend many hours inside watching violent movies and playing graphic video games.

3 **Children are more apt to be exposed to sexual images and pornography indoors.** Again, they see a lot on television and more and more children are viewing pornography on the computer. They'll see more 'sex' inside than out.

4 **There's more sexual and physical abuse indoors.** Studies find that children are more apt to be physically and sexually abused by family members and/or relatives, (or, in many cases, step-parents) than by strangers. In *Paranoid Parenting*, Furedi notes, "David Finklehor, director of Crimes Against Children research center at the University of New Hampshire, claims that the biggest perils are close at hand; between 50-100 kids are killed a year by strangers, whereas there are one thousand kids killed each year by parents."

5 **Family members, not strangers are doing most of the abductions and kidnappings.** Richard Louv, in an interview with *Education News*, noted, "Now consider the facts about stranger-danger. Child abductions by strangers are, in fact, growing rarer. Nationwide, 200 to 300 children were abducted by strangers in 1988, compared with 115 children in 1999. By a wide margin, family members, not strangers, are the most common kidnappers. New York State's Division of Criminal Justice Services' 2004 annual report on missing children notes that the overwhelming majority of missing children cases were reported as suspected runaways."

6 **The more time indoors, the more likely a child will become overweight and get diabetes.** When children are inside, they are sedentary. When they are outdoors they are active, burning off calories. Also, the more time children sit in front of televisions and computers, the more likely they are loading up on junk food. Recent research done at Temple University and Penn found that obese kids are absent more at school. Researchers looked at 1,069 fourth-to sixth-graders for one academic year in nine Philadelphia schools. Of 180 school days, researchers found on average the normal weight students missed 10.1 days, overweight kids missed 10.9 days and obese children missed 12.2 days. The study revealed one other fascinating fact: underweight children had the fewest absences—7.5 on average.

7 **Gross motor skills seldom are developed indoors.** Kids need to hop, skip, run, and jump.

8 **Senses are dulled inside.** The more time children are outside, the more they enhance their sense of smell, touch, taste, and hearing.

9 **The more time indoors, the more sleeping problems.** Children who spend a lot of time outdoors seldom have difficulties falling to sleep at night.

10 **The great outdoors helps improve one's attention problems.** Research studies by the Human-Environmental Research Laboratory at the University of Illinois show that direct exposure to nature relieves some of the symptoms of attention-deficit hyperactivity disorders.

11 **Less stress.** For both children and adults, being outside is a great stress-releaser.

12 **Outdoor classes enhance learning.** Several recent articles are telling us that students who had many classes outside improved their test scores.

13 **Social skills are improved outdoors.** How can children learn strategies for getting along with others if they spend all their time inside? Outdoor kids learn more about winning and losing, sharing, dealing with the neighborhood bully, taking turns, and working together. I think children learn more problem-solving skills outside, than inside.

14 **Outdoor kids are more creative.** Think back to when you were young and spent time outside. You invented games, built forts, climbed trees, collected rocks and bugs, played with dandelions, and invented bizarre gadgets.

15 **Outdoor kids have more respect for animals and the environment.** The more time kids are exposed to trees, rivers, mountains, streams, lakes, and animals, the more apt they will engage in environmental issues when they get older.

16 **Serotonin levels are increased with exposure to the sun.** Serotonin is a chemical substance that is derived from the amino acid trypothan. It occurs in the brain. People with low levels of this chemical are more likely to be depressed, irritable, disruptive, or aggressive. One of the best sources of serotonin is the sun. Exercise and eating a lot of vegetables also helps. But so many kids aren't in the sun, or exercising, or eating enough vegetables. In his book, *Living with our Genes*, Dean Hamer tells how a lack of serotonin leads children to load up on junk food.

Judith Wurthman, head of the Nutrition and Behavior Studies Group at MIT, believes there are two types of hunger; physical hunger, which is a response to the body's need for nourishment, and psychological hunger, which is propelled by our need for comfort and solace. The key to psychological hunger, according to Wurthman, is serotonin—the same neurotransmitter involved in the personality traits of neuroticism and harm avoidance, aggression and hostility. Serotonin is the key chemical involved in feeling depressed, anxious, tense, irritable, frustrated, angry, stressed and mentally exhausted. Physical hunger can be satisfied by eating a wide range of nutritious foods; psychological hunger can be satisfied with foods that supply serotonin. For people with these kinds of cravings, it would seem logical to eat high-serotonin foods, or better yet, a no-calorie serotonin pill. The problem is that serotonin can't pass directly from the bloodstream into the brain. Instead, the body needs sweet and starchy carbohydrates to boost the brain's supply of tryptophan, the amino acid building block for serotonin. There's always room on the carbohydrate train, which is why when you feel down or depressed, the first food that comes to mind is a cookie, piece of cake, or potato chips.

17 Indoor bullying is worse than outdoor bullying.

Cyberbullying, a fairly new term, is when a child, preteen, or teen is tormented, threatened, harassed, humiliated, embarrassed, or otherwise targeted by another child, preteen, or teen using the Internet, interactive and digital technologies or mobile phone. According to the National Crime Prevention Council, kids bully online by:

❖ Sending someone mean or threatening emails, instant messages, or text messages.

❖ Excluding someone from an instant messenger buddy list or blocking their email for no reason.

❖ Tricking someone into revealing personal or embarrassing information and sending it to others.

❖ Breaking into someone's email or instant message account to send cruel or untrue messages while posing as that person.

- ❖ Creating websites to make fun of another person such as a classmate or teacher.

- ❖ Using websites to rate peers as prettiest, ugliest, etc.

The NCPC adds, "Victims of cyberbullying may experience many of the same effects as children who are bullied in person, such as a drop in grades, low self-esteem, a change in interests, or depression. However, cyberbullying can seem more extreme to its victims because of several factors:"

- ❖ Occurs in children's homes. Being bullied at home can take away the place children feel most safe.

- ❖ Can be harsher. Often kids say things online that they wouldn't say in person, mainly because they can't see the other person's reaction.

- ❖ Far reaching. Kids can send emails making fun of someone to their entire class or school with a few clicks, or post them on a website for the whole world to see.

- ❖ Anonymity. Cyberbullies often hide behind screen names and email addresses that don't identify who they are. Not knowing who is responsible for bullying messages can add to a victim's insecurity.

- ❖ May be inescapable. It may seem easy to get away from a cyberbully—just get offline—but for some kids, not going online takes away one of the major places they socialize.

18 **More serious injuries occur inside.** In 2004, according to Safe Kids Worldwide, 5,359 children died from unintentional injuries in the United States. The six most common causes of death were burns, suffocation, drowning, choking, falls and poisoning.

These words, spoken over a hundred years ago by horticultur-
ist Luther Burbank, still hold true today, "Every child should
have mud pies, grasshoppers, water bugs, tadpoles, frogs, mud-
turtles, elderberries, wild strawberries, acorns, chestnuts, trees to
climb, brooks to wade in, water lilies, bats, bees, various animals
to pet, hayfields, pine cones, rocks to roll, sand, snakes, huckle-
berries, and hornets; any child who has been deprived of these
has been deprived of the best part of education." Get outdoors
with your kids and enjoy these things. Richard Louv reminds us,
"One of the most important gifts a parent or teacher can give a
child is his or her own infectious enthusiasm for the outdoors."

Sleep: "Bed is a medicine."—Italian adage

William Dement, one of the top sleep researchers in the country said, "If Americans and Europeans would simply go to bed
an hour earlier each night, and turn off the television no later
than an hour before that, Western society would be happier and
healthier." Oh, so true! We all could benefit from more sleep.
According to Gregg Easterbrook in his book, *The Progress
Paradox*, "Studies show that the typical American sleeps an
hour less per night than a generation ago, two to three less per
night than was standard in previous centuries. Ten hours per
night of sleep has probably been the norm for most of human
history; today, in the United States, the norm is seven hours." It
appears that people living hundreds of years ago knew more
about the importance of sleep than we do today. In the 1691
book, *The Whole of Man*, the author wrote, "Sleep's purpose is
to restore our frail bodies, to make us more profitable spiritually and materially, and not for idle."

Inadequate sleep can cause **decreases** in: performance, con-
centration, reaction times, consolidation of information, and
learning. Inadequate sleep can cause **increases** in: memory laps-
es, accidents and injuries, behavior problems, and mood problems. Surgeon and consumer advocate, Dr. Sam Speron notes,
"Without enough sleep, a person has trouble focusing and

responding quickly. There is also growing evidence linking a chronic lack of sleep with an increased risk of obesity, diabetes, heart disease and infections."

In order to have GRIT, people need sleep. They need enough energy to exercise, study, help others, and be productive citizens. But how much sleep is actually needed? How many hours should you get? What about elementary students compared to high school students? A great read is the book, *At Day's Close: Night in Times Past*. The author, A. Roger Ekirch, explored many of the early theories of sleep. Here are a few of the more interesting ones that were recognized in the 1500-1700's:

Six hours sleep for man, seven
for a woman, and eight for a fool.

Nature requires five, custom takes seven,
laziness nine, and wickedness eleven.

To sup at six and go to bed at ten,
will make a man live ten times ten.

Sleep eight hours in the summer and nine
hours during long winter evenings.

Early to bed and early to rise makes
a man healthy, wealthy, and wise.
–Benjamin Franklin

According to the latest information from the National Institute of Health, "Sleep needs vary from person to person and change throughout life. For example, newborns sleep 16-18 hours a day, children in preschool sleep 10 to 12 hours a day, and school-aged children and teens need at least 9 hours of sleep a day. Adults, including seniors, need 7 to 8 hours sleep each day." Many adults struggle to get their needed rest, but I'm getting very concerned about school-aged children's lack of sleep. Check out these notes from a recent survey completed by the

Sleep Foundation that focused on children aged 11-17:

- ❖ Some 28 percent of high school students said they fell asleep in class at least once a week.

- ❖ 22 percent dozed off doing homework.

- ❖ 14 percent arrive late or miss school because they oversleep.

- ❖ More than half of adolescent drivers have driven while drowsy.

- ❖ 28% said they were too tired to exercise.

- ❖ Just 20% said they get nine hours of sleep on school nights.

It's time to take sleep serious! Following are twelve strategies that can help you and our youth catch a few more z's every night.

A DOZEN Z's TIPS

1 **Get physical.** Regular vigorous exercise enhances sleep.

2 **Get outdoors.** Children who spend a lot of time playing or working outdoors fall asleep quicker than children who sit in front of the television all evening.

3 **Wind-down the last half-hour.** The last 30 minutes before hitting the sack are vital. Read, pray, work on a puzzle, or share positive conversations.

4 **Limit television viewing the last hour before bed.** Gregg Easterbrook writes in his book, *The Progress Paradox*, "Those who watch television until lights-out tend to have less deep sleep than those who engage in a quiet activity, because television is full of choppy images, flashes, explosions, shouting, crying, gunplay, superficial sexuality, adversity both real and simulated. Viewing such disquieting material before nodding off prevents the mind from calming fully for sleep." I've surveyed hundreds of students during the past few years, over two-thirds tell me they have a hard time falling asleep. They go to bed on time but often take two or three hours to fall asleep.

5 **Remove electronic items from the bedroom.** This may seem a bit radical. The Sleep Foundation tells us, "Nearly 97% of all youngsters have at least one electronic item in their bedroom such as television, computer, phone or music device. Adolescents with four or more such items in their bedrooms are much more likely than their peers to get an insufficient amount of sleep at night."

6 **Utilize a sound machine.** Consider placing an aquarium or a device that makes calming sounds like the wind blowing, rain falling, or waves rolling, in the bedroom to drown outside noises.

7 **Sprinkle lavender on the pillow.** The pleasant odor helps to induce sleep.

8 **Have a cup of chamomile tea or warm milk.** Chamomile is one of the safest medicinal herbs. It is a soothing, non-caffeinated, gentle relaxant that has a satisfying, apple-like aroma and flavor. Warm milk is rich in tryptophan, which is converted to serotonin, which can aid relaxation.

9 **Eat lightly.** Heavy meals and caffeine a couple hours before bed is not good!

10 **Turn down the volume in the house.** When the children go to bed, parents need to turn down the television and lower their voices.

11 **Cool it.** Most people sleep better when the bedroom is cool.

12 **Husbands and wives must support each other.** Raising children, running a household, and going to work every day makes it very difficult to get your eight hours of sleep. Both parents need to do their 'fair share' keeping things going in the home (household chores, discipline issues with children, running errands, help with homework, etc). Spouses need to get creative with helping each other get enough sleep. For example, dad could get up early on Saturday morning to keep an eye on the kids while mom gets a couple extra hours of sleep. Then mom could return the favor on Sunday morning.

KEEP LEARNING.

As we continue our exploration of the 'inner self,' (the things we have almost complete control of) I have to stress the importance of learning. Gritty individuals show responsibility for their education/learning; they realize the importance of constantly feeding their brains. Gandhi said, "Live as if you were to die tomorrow. Learn as if you were to live forever." There is a great story in John Tayman's book, *The Colony*, about a young man with leprosy who was dying. The young man, Harada, was a very intelligent man who had graduated with honors from college. One day a friend asked Harada about the changes in his reading habits. Harada responded, "I've stopped reading books. Now I only read magazines. There isn't much point in trying to keep on learning." Are you a magazine reader or a book reader? Are you tenacious about learning new things? I once read about a 108 year-old freed slave who wanted to learn how to read the Bible before she died. Then there's Eric Hoffer. This famous author mysteriously went blind when he was seven years of age. He unexpectedly regained his sight at age fifteen. He was so afraid that blindness would return that he became obsessed with reading. He continued to read one book after another.

As you can probably tell by now, I believe that reading is the key to learning. Unfortunately there is a present day trend of people reading fewer books. An ABC News item noted that 27% of Americans said they did not even read one book in 2006! In a July 16, 2007 article in *ednews.org*, H. Bernard Wechsler reported, "A 5-year study of the reading habits of 1,050 high school and college students and 875 executives reveals reading books is last on their hierarchy of values. It is an old fashioned knowledge technology. These results mirror the past twenty years of information technology. Public access to the Internet is a form of neuroplasticity. The computer changes not just our learning habits, but the function and structure of the brain of Homo sapiens." Wechsler's article uncovered this amazing fact: "The book publishing industry confirms the typical executive (college graduate) reads only one book annually!"

WHY WE NEED TO KEEP READING

❖ Reading keeps you updated on current events. It will help you carry on intelligent conversations with others.

❖ Reading is exciting; you learn new things! Concentrate on more non-fiction for a while.

❖ Reading improves attention span.

❖ Reading helps eliminate stress and anxieties. It is so relaxing to find a quiet place to read a great book!

❖ Reading a book, as compared to scanning the Internet, does much to help improve comprehension and vocabulary skills.

❖ Reading enhances creativity.

❖ And most importantly, what a great modeling tool for children. Research shows that kids who read a lot usually have parents who read a lot. How often do you and your children visit the library and book store?

Where do you stand on this topic? Are you happy with your spirituality? Do you regularly attend the religious institution of your choice? Do you encourage your children to attend? Do you enhance your spirit by reading the Bible or other religious writings? Do you feel more spiritual sitting in a church or resting on a beautiful mountain side? Regardless of your beliefs and actions, your spirituality is another aspect of your inner-self that you can control. You can choose your belief system.

In my book, *Keeping Love Alive in the Family*, I addressed the topic of spiritual wellness. I explored research done by Stinnett and Defrain in 1986. These researchers found that strong families considered spiritual wellness **the** unifying force; it held the family together. Also, in my book I discovered that people expressed their spiritual wellness in various ways. They may stick to a strict value system that aims at helping others. They feel they have an important purpose in life. They may also believe in or have awareness of a higher power. Some express their spiritual wellness by trying to make the world a better place. Others often express a feeling of optimism, or feel they are part of something that is so much greater than they are. Many families join churches, synagogues, or temples and attend on a regular basis, while others focus on prayer or meditation.

A few years ago I asked Reverend David Harvin, a United Methodist Church pastor, about the important role of the church in today's society.

The church is one of the few places left in our society that constantly gives a strong message about the family. Families are good. They are where important nurturing takes place. Families are the primary way God works in the world to help children grow. The church has come to understand that families may be single, grandparent and child, or couples without children, as well as the traditional nuclear family. In a world where so many messages urge people not to take responsibility towards others, the church brings a message of moral value to those who function as families. Many families have moved away from regular church attendance, but those families that do attend seem to get a source of strength from the involvement. Church life not only talks about values, it offers opportunities for service such as painting a child care center, gathering food for the hungry, or raising funds for a well in a third world country. Church life can be an enriching and encouraging place for families in this stressful, modern world.

THE OUTER-SELF

"The basics of a decent, civilized life are timeless;
get up early in the morning, take reasonable care
of your body, mind, and soul; do some kind of work
that benefits the world instead of harms it; respect and
cherish other people; and then get some sleep."
—Bo Lozoff

Our outer-self encompasses those things in life in which we do not have total control of, but we can have a major impact. We are responsible to take care of the environment and get involved in our communities. As parents it is our responsibility to take care of our children and to teach them how to be responsible. Husbands and wives need to be supportive of each other, to share household tasks, manage finances, spend quality time together, and respect each other's 'alone' time to pursue hobbies and interests. Once again, I cannot stress enough the importance of adults modeling responsibility. Author, Robert Fulghum, said, "Don't worry that children never listen to you, worry that they are always watching you."

There are three basic parenting styles: permissive, authoritarian, and authoritative. (Notice that these three are closely related to teaching styles). Permissive parents tend to be slaves to their children and allow them to regulate their own behaviors/actions; they give kids too much freedom. Authoritarian parents tend to be too strict and attempt to shape and control all aspects of their children's behavior. Authoritative parenting tends to be democratic in nature and involves setting fair, firm limits on their children's behavior, and use reasonable, natural and logical consequences. Parenting expert, Kevin Leman, paints a clearer picture of the different styles, "The authoritative parent stands on the solid middle ground between the extremes of permissiveness and authoritarianism. Neither the permissive nor the authoritarian parent helps the child learn to make decisions. The permissive parent robs the child of self-respect and a sense of initiative by doing so much **for** him. The authoritarian parent robs the child of self-esteem and a sense of independence by doing so much **to** him." Author, Laurence Steinberg adds, "Virtually, regardless of their family background, adolescents whose parents are warm, firm, and democratic enjoy psychological and behavioral advantages over their peers."

Authoritative, democratic parents tend to raise children who are more self-disciplined and responsible. Whenever parents and teachers have to discipline a child, they need to ask themselves, "How will my actions help the child become more responsible?" In my opinion, the best way for adults to help young people be more responsible for their actions is to eliminate the word, *why.*

When a child misbehaves or fails to live up to his responsibilities (chores, homework, behavior) don't ask, "Why?" By asking this question, you are inviting the child to come up an excuse to justify his action. For instance, if you saw John hit his sister and you say, "John, why did you hit your sister?" he will probably say something like, "She called me a name!" Rarely is there a valid reason for hitting. Your reaction to his hitting should focus on the word *what*, instead of *why*. By using *what* you are helping him take more responsibility for his action. Respond with these questions: *What did you just do? What is the rule about hitting in this house? What have I told you to do if she teases you? What else could you have done instead of hitting?* Follow through with an appropriate consequence. Effective teachers have learned to avoid the *why* word. Seldom will you hear a teacher ask, "Why don't you have your homework?" Students can come up with some clever responses to that question. There is a Sufi saying that goes, "Self-justification is worse than the original offense."

CHORES AND SHARED TASKS

Everyone in the family needs to do his or her fair share to keep things running as smoothly as possible. If things get out of balance, for instance one person seems to be doing most of the work, conflicts occur. Here are a few suggestions to help build responsibility in the family.

❖ Keep this saying in mind, "A house needs to be clean enough to be healthy and dirty enough to be happy." Some parents operate the home like a museum. So much time and energy goes into keeping the house spotless, the 'fun' is missing. A happy home gets a bit messy at times with toys on the floor, dog hair on the couch, and a few dirty dishes in the sink.

❖ Recent studies on marriage find that husband/wife relationships are strong when they share household tasks (washing dishes, disciplining children, homework issues). Children need to see dad washing dishes once in a while.

❖ Household chores should be balanced as much as possible between parents and children.

❖ Children's allowances **must not** be tied to chores! Why should children be given money for taking out the trash or washing dishes? They need to realize that one of their responsibilities is to do their fair share. If children do not complete chores, use logical consequences. For special, lengthier chores such as raking leaves or cleaning out the garage, a little financial incentive is appropriate at times.

FAMILY FINANCES AND ALLOWANCES

Being financially responsible is not easy. Obviously, single people are solely in charge of their finances. They have to monitor charge cards, pay bills, save money, and make major purchases (car, house, etc). Husbands and wives need to have equal input into family finances, regardless if one or both spouses have jobs outside the house. My experience as a marriage counselor helped me realize that one of the major areas of conflict between husbands and wives dealt with financial issues.

As far as children are concerned, probably the best way to help them learn about being responsible with money is through allowances. Consider giving children a small weekly allowance, not tied to chores. Parents need to agree on an amount based on the ages of their children. Once children have money, they'll begin to learn how to spend and save. Remember, once you give them their allowances, they decide what to do with it. They may run out and buy a cheap toy, or they may decide to save it for a bigger purchase. I do recommend that parents encourage children to save, give ten percent to church, or donate a small amount to a charity.

HOBBIES, INTERESTS, EXTRA-CURRICULAR ACTIVITIES

Young people who get involved in positive after-school activities and who are very passionate about their hobbies and interests, not only stay out of major trouble, they also learn numerous life skills that build responsibility. They have to attend meetings, practices, deal with different coaches and leaders, find time to get schoolwork completed, and squeeze in quality family time. As adults we need to do all we can to keep children busy and to support them. This includes taking them to practice, paying registration fees, buying supplies, and attending their games and performances. Show sincere interest in their activities. There is an Amish saying, "Take interest in your children's interests or they will lose interest in their interests." And, always be there. There is no better way to show interest, love, and support than cheering from the sidelines. My father worked rotating shifts in a paper mill (7am-3pm, 3pm-11pm, 11pm-7am), but whenever I had a game in high school, he was able to adjust his schedule, trade shifts with someone, or 'sneak out' for an hour or two to root me on. What a great feeling it was to look up in the stands and see him.

Spouses need to support each others' hobbies and interests. Author, psychologist, John O'Donohue suggests that couples should allow each other their time alone. He calls this 'time alone' or 'away' as their "Wilderness Territory." My Wilderness Territory is running and my wife respects it. She knows that almost every day after work I go running before dinner. Some days I'll get up early for a long run, while once or twice a month I'll head out of town for the day to race. One of her territories is working in the yard with her plants, flowers, and trees. I know how important this is to her.

COMMUNITY INVOLVEMENT

We need to take responsibility for our communities. Get involved in the schools. Find time to volunteer, give blood, or deliver meals to the homeless. Take your children and let them witness the benefits of helping others. Attend local government meetings, read the newspaper and vote. Find time to visit neighbors and set up a community watch program. Grow a few extra vegetables in the garden and give them to the family next door.

How about coaching the girl's softball team or helping with your church's Vacation Bible School?

ENVIRONMENTAL ISSUES

Getting involved in your community is important, but don't forget world-wide issues such as pollution, global warming, recycling, and respecting animals and nature. Children must see us addressing these vital issues. We all have to take some responsibility for our beautiful planet.

CHAPTER 4
INTEGRITY

"In looking for people to hire, look for three qualities:
integrity, intelligence, and energy. And if they don't
have the first, the other two will kill you."
—Warren Buffet, American financier

DO THE RIGHT THING!

I've looked over hundreds of quotes on integrity and I discovered that the words *do the right thing* are used quite often. Here are a few:

"Have the courage to say no. Have the courage
to face the truth. Do the right thing because it is right.
These are the magic keys to living with integrity."
—W. Clement Stone

"Integrity is doing the right thing,
even if nobody is watching."
—Anonymous

"The time is always right to do what is right."
—Martin Luther King, Jr.

"Real integrity is doing the right thing, knowing that nobody's going to know whether you did it or not."
—Oprah Winfrey

"Quality means doing it right when no one is looking."
—Henry Ford

"Keep true, never be ashamed of doing right, decide on what you think is right, and stick to it!"
—George Eliot

"As a leader, you not only have to do the right thing, but be perceived to be doing the right thing. A consequence of seeking a leadership position is being put under intense public scrutiny, being held to high standards, and enhancing a reputation that is constantly under threat."
—Jeffrey Sonnenfeld

Unfortunately we are bombarded daily with news items of politicians, celebrities, religious leaders, and professional athletes not doing the right thing. Our young people hear of politicians misappropriating funds or committing adultery. They also learn of pop singers who have been arrested for DUI or others who boast of being married for just one day. Hip-hop stars blast vulgar lyrics and brag about the number of times they've been shot or arrested. Children watch the news and discover their sports heroes involved in steroid use, doping, betting on games, or encouraging disgusting activities such as dog fighting. Even a few Christian leaders have been involved in drug use, soliciting prostitutes, and abusing children. How do you help your children understand what is happening? How do you make sense of it all?

Have you even been disappointed in the actions of one of your favorite athletes, politicians, or religious leaders? What emotions do you feel when you read about teachers, police officers, religious leaders, or government officials who lack integrity? Usually my first reaction is anger. I think, "How could he or she do that?" Here are three personal examples.

* ❖ Several years ago I read a remarkable non-fiction book, *The Blood Runs Like a River Through my Dreams.* I remember telling my wife that it was one of the best books I'd ever read! A couple years later it was found that the author, Nasdijj, had made-up the whole story; he lied. I was so upset I wanted to find him and give him a piece of my mind!

* ❖ I read an article in the newspaper about some football coaches in northern Virginia. It seems that they decided not to do the usual post game ritual of having the opposing teams shake hands because there was too much 'trash-talking' and a few fights. Instead of having the coaches teach the players self-discipline, sportsmanship, and integrity, they decided to eliminate the ritual! How does this help the players grow to be respectful individuals?

* ❖ Here is an example of how some governments show little integrity for their soldiers. Here in our country there have been reports of soldiers who returned from Iraq and Afghanistan with injuries that were not getting good health care. They risked their lives for us, we need to treat them like heroes and provide them with the best of care! One of the worse cases in history of neglecting war heroes took place in Russia in World War II. In the book, *A Writer at War*, Antony Beever, tells how Soviet soldiers would rather be killed than return home as a cripple. He writes, "The prospect of being mutilated or becoming a cripple always represented a far greater fear for Soviet soldiers than being killed. There was of course the unshakeable belief that a woman would never want to look at them again. This may have been a misleading male nightmare, but the true awfulness of their fate did not become apparent until after the war when maimed and crippled Red

Army soldiers were treated with unbelievable callousness by the Soviet authorities. Those reduced to a trunk with stumps were known as *samovars*. After the war they were rounded up and sent to towns in the Arctic Circle so that the Soviet capital would not be made unsightly with limbless veterans."

YOU CAN'T HAVE
INTE*GRIT*Y
WITHOUT THE G-R-I-T

One day while I was doing a GRIT lesson with second graders, a boy raised his hand and said, "Mr. Carr, do you know the word grit is hidden in the word integrity?" I hadn't noticed that before! Earlier in this book I wrote, "It takes grit to be fit." Well, thanks to the second grader, I'm here to tell you, "You can't have integrity without grit." It isn't always easy to do the right thing. Almost every day of our lives we face difficult situations in which we have to ask ourselves, "What is the right thing to do?"

Well, what **is** the right thing to do? Whenever I ask that question to parents, students, and teachers, I tend to hear these familiar responses: be honest, tell the truth, don't lie, don't cheat, keep your word, help those less fortunate, always be there for your friends and family, be kind, be compassionate, don't hurt others, use good manners, don't boast or gossip, work hard, do your best, learn to forgive, don't seek revenge, follows rules and laws, don't steal, share your belongings, take care of animals and our environment and practice what you preach.

Many people mention the word 'sincere' as it relates to integrity. We want others to be sincere. Author Mark Nepo, in his book, *The Exquisite Risk*, tells us the origin of the word sincere; it is rather interesting! "If we trace the word itself, we return to Roman times, where the Western form of the word originated. It comes from the Latin *sin cere*, meaning 'without wax.' During the Italian Renaissance, sculptors were as plentiful as plumbers, and markets selling marble and other stones were as prevalent as hardware stores. Frequently, stone sellers would fill the cracks in flawed stones with wax and try to sell them as flawless. Thus, an honest stone seller became known as someone who was sincere—one who showed his stone without wax, cracks, and all." Don't hide your flaws! Nobody is perfect.

One strategy that helps me 'do the right thing' is I imagine that my wife, children, and students are always watching me, and if I do slip once in a while, I don't feel good. Ezra Taft Benson says, "You cannot do wrong and feel right. It is impossible." As we struggle to be people of integrity, we must also do what we can to help our young people develop this positive trait. The following suggestions should help.

TIPS FOR NURTURING CHILDREN'S INTEGRITY

1 **Show them integrity.** Children must witness honesty, sincerity, and kindness from parents, teachers, and other important adults in their lives. A study completed by Jonathan Haidt at the University of Virginia found that people who witnessed acts of kindness, loyalty, and heroism were motivated to help others. Haidt also found that, not only do 'observers' of integrity pass it on, they experience physiological benefits such as a sense of "elevation." They felt warm, open, glowing feelings in the chest. In other words, when people witnessed kindness, it made them feel better and motivated them to do good things. Model integrity!

2 **Teach them the difference between right and wrong.** Believe it or not, many children don't know the difference because our society is giving them too many mixed messages. When a child is faced with a dilemma, ask, "What is the right thing to do?" Present them with scenarios or stories without endings and have them brainstorm positive solutions.

3 **Use concrete language.** These days it seems that we are afraid to 'tell it like it is.' Just listen to the news to see what I mean. *The senator had a memory lapse.* (He lied!) *The hospital administrator was a shoddy bookkeeper.* (She embezzled!) *The student inflated her GPA.* (She was dishonest!) *The author failed to report much of his earnings on his tax report.* (He cheated the government!) *She intentionally deceived the banker.* (She committed fraud!) *The teen signed her mother's name on the check and cashed it.* (She committed forgery!). Don't be hesitant to use the words 'right' and 'wrong.' When Janet steals, say, "That's wrong; stealing is wrong!" If Louis cheats in a table game, tell him, "Cheating is wrong!" Young children need to be constantly reminded about 'right' and 'wrong.' Try to avoid the terms 'good' and 'bad.' Don't say, "Mike, you did a bad thing," say "You did the wrong thing." Don't say, "You are bad!" say, "What you did was wrong." When children make poor choices, focus on their behaviors, and not what kind of person they are. "Joey, you are not a bad person, but what you did was not good."

4 **Use teachable moments.** If you are driving along the interstate with your seven-year-old daughter and you see someone in the car ahead of you throw trash out the window, do you say anything to her? She needs to hear you say, "That was wrong! It is against the law and it hurts the environment." If you and your son are watching a movie in which a man hits his wife, do you say anything?

5 **Be careful with praise.** Try to avoid dishing out too much praise when you observe children doing the right thing. Remember, our goal when working with young people is to have them do the right thing, because it **is** the right thing to do, not because they'll get a treat or praise. Many parents and teachers are giving out "goodies" when children are caught being good. As mentioned earlier in this book, research by Alfie Kohn and others found that many children will **not** always do the right things once the "goodies" are eliminated. I want my students to open the door for an elderly person because it is right, not because they hope to get a pat on the back and a sticker! A little verbal praise once in a while is fine, but better yet, acknowledge rather than praise. For instance, instead of saying, "Maureen, I'm so proud of you for picking up your toys without being told," say, "I noticed you picked up your toys without being told."

6 **Read 'em their rights!** Encourage children to closely monitor their whereabouts and actions. At school I post several of these signs in various locations (bathrooms, halls, media center, etc).

Am I:

In the *RIGHT* place

At the *RIGHT* time

With the *RIGHT* people

Doing the *RIGHT* thing?

7 **Tell them tales of integrity.** Storytelling is a powerful tool. Children will remember stories better than lessons. Focus on true stories. Here are a few of my favorites.

TEN TALES OF INTEGRITY

ROBERTO CLEMENTE'S MISSION

Roberto Clemente is considered one of the greatest baseball players ever to play in the major leagues. He played eighteen years with the Pittsburgh Pirates. He was selected for the All Star Game several times and in 1966 he was voted as the Most Valuable Player in the National League. He was born in Puerto Rico and he never forgot his roots. He often donated his time and money to supply young Latin Americans with baseball equipment and food. Almost every off-season he was involved in charity work. In the last game of the 1972 season he joined an exclusive group of major leaguers when he got his 3,000th career hit. Later that year a massive earthquake hit Nicaragua. Clemente had to help! He donated money and secured supplies from companies. He had the relief assistance flown to the needy people. He soon learned that aid packages on the first two flights had been diverted by corrupt officials, never reaching victims. He decided to accompany the next flight to make sure relief got there. The plane was overloaded with supplies and crashed. His body was never found.

NOT YOUR AVERAGE MAIL CARRIER

In the late 1930's Addie Clawson was hired as the new mail carrier in the rural mountains near Boone, North Carolina. Regardless of the weather, she made sure people got their mail. Many days she had to navigate mud roads, fallen trees, snow-drifts and flooded paths. She knew people relied on her to get letters delivered; she rarely let them down. Besides being reli-able, she was very compassionate. She often checked on the old folks, delivered medications, and picked up groceries for those who didn't have a car. On Christmas Eve she often made extra trips to make sure presents got under the tree on time. Addie did another neat thing. On her travels she noticed how disappointed children got when they didn't receive any mail, so she and her daughters would write them letters! Addie was so appreciated that she would often find gifts and treats in mail boxes. People would leave her baked goods, fruit, vegetables, and presents.

Addie's remarkable tale comes from Julia Taylor Ebel's book, *Addie Clawson, Appalachian Mail Carrier.*

INTEGRITY TO THE END OF LIFE

Marie-Antoinette (1755-1793) was Queen of France. She married Louis XVI of France in 1790. Many historians believe her incredible extravagances were deemed to be partly responsible for the French Revolution. Other historians write about her kindness and compassion. Both she and her husband were guillotined. She maintained dignity and politeness to the very end. According to one source her last words were, "Sir, forgive me, I did not do it deliberately." Apparently, while on the scaffold, she accidentally stepped on the executioner's foot!

A VALUABLE LESSON FROM BOOKER T. WASHINGTON

Booker T. Washington, the great black educator, founded the Tuskegee Institute in Alabama in the 1880's. I'm sure he taught many lessons at the institute, but his most important lesson was taught, not in a classroom, but while walking along a road.

Although President Lincoln had abolished slavery in the 1860's, many blacks were still being mistreated twenty years later. One day, Booker T. Washington was passing a beautiful mansion owned by a wealthy white family. The mistress of the house saw him walking by. She didn't recognize him and yelled, "Hey, you! Come chop me a pile of firewood right now!" He could have gotten angry and replied, "No," but he didn't. Instead he calmly removed his jacket and rolled up his sleeves.

He picked up the ax and went to work. Several hours later he went back to the house to inform the lady that he was finished. He handed her the ax and left. She never thanked him. As he was leaving, one of her servants said, "Ma'am, that man was Professor Washington!"

The next day the embarrassed mistress went to Washington to apologize. He responded, "It's entirely all right, Madam. I like to work, and I'm delighted to do favors for my friends." He found a new friend, and she ended up donating thousands of dollars to his needy institute. His integrity paid off.

ELLEN KEEPS HER PROMISE

The Smith family left Missouri on the Overland Trail and headed west. They were in a wagon train that started with 300 wagons. Sickness took over the camp and many died from typhoid fever, yet William Smith's family continued along the trail. His daughter, Louisa, age sixteen, became gravely ill with the fever. The stress of the travel and the worries of his ill daughter led him to suffer a heart attack and die. He left his wife Ellen and nine children to go on without him. As Ellen urged her family on, Louisa's illness continued to worsen. Louisa was in so much pain that the family packed a pillow and blanket on an ox, making a more comfortable bed for her on the bumpy roads. Louisa knew she was going to die soon and told her mother to promise her that they bury her in a grave at least six feet deep so the wolves wouldn't dig her up and eat her. She also wanted a pile of rocks on top of her grave as further protection against the hungry wolves. When Louisa died, Ellen and a few men started digging the grave, but the men stopped digging after reaching a depth of only four feet. Ellen had to keep her promise as she urged the men to continue. When they refused, she continued and several hours later she completed the six-foot hole in the ground. Louisa was buried with a large pile of rocks on top of her grave.

KEEPING THEIR VOWS

In today's world when there are so many couples not keep their wedding vows and promises, I love to hear stories like this one. In the early 1900's Dr. Henry Holland traveled from England to provide medical services to the poor in India and Pakistan. One of his services was to do simple cataract surgery on blind people, restoring their sight. There was a married couple, both blinded by cataract for many years that stayed together through the ordeal. Although they were loving and supportive, they hadn't seen each other's face in a long, long time. Dr. Holland performed surgery on the couple and placed bandages on their faces to allow time for the eyes to heal. Later, he had the couple stand face-to-face as he removed the bandages simultaneously. The husband and wife stared at each other for a long time with tears flowing. Dr. Holland said they looked like a couple falling in love for the first time.

IT'S ALMOST MIDNIGHT

One important characteristic of integrity is honesty. We should always be honest with others, but are we always honest with ourselves? In the January, 2006 issue of *Runner's World*, there was an excellent story of a runner who faced an integrity dilemma. Adam Cohen, a long distance runner, had set a personal goal of running 2,000 miles in the year 2000. At 11:08pm on December 31, he sat down to review his yearly running log and to celebrate his accomplishment; he ran 2,000 miles! But wait. He added up the miles again and realized he was three miles short! Oh, no; he had only 1,997 miles. He looked out the window; it was cold and dark. He had to complete his goal. His wife thought he was crazy as he laced up his running shoes and headed out in the dark. He ran the three miles and finished five minutes before midnight. He did it! No one else would have known that he was three miles short, but Adam would have known it; he had to be honest with himself.

RUNNING UP THE ROCKY STEPS

The steps leading up to the Philadelphia Museum of Art are probably the most famous steps in the United States. Most Americans have seen at least one of Sylvester Stallone's popular *Rocky* boxing movies. In the first movie, Rocky runs up the seventy-two steps, raises his arms, and feels he is ready to fight the champion. The movie and the running up the steps scene have been great motivators for others. Every day in Philadelphia hundreds of people run, walk, or crawl up the steps. Author Michael Vitez wrote a book about some of these stair climbers: *Rocky Stories*. He interviewed one such man, Latone Allen, who runs up and down the steps ten times every morning, no matter the weather, at 5:30. He is a single parent who wants his two boys to have a good life. His daily ritual motivates him to get out and do his best. He notes, "My dream is to see my kids have a better life than I have, with fewer struggles. The stairs help me do that. In my job as a loan officer, if I feel good, then I produce better, and I perform better, and then I can do better for my kids. So I come to the steps for me and my family."

TESTING GRANDFATHER'S BELIEFS

In their 2007 book, *Moved by the Spirit*, Jeffrey Kottler and Jon Carlson share several fascinating stories in the lives of leaders. In one story, Arun Gandhi, grandson of the late Indian spiritual and political leader Mahatma Gandhi, learned a valuable life lesson. Arun was a very angry, rebellious boy. At the age of twelve his father sent him to live with his grandfather, Mahatma, hoping the spiritual leader could have a positive affect on the boy. During the last two years of his life, Mahatma needed money to assist him in his peaceful pursuits. He decided to charge a small fee of 5 rupees for his autograph. Arun was given the job of greeting visitors, collecting rupees, and gathering materials that people wanted autographed. Arun was angry because he didn't think he should have to pay for his grandfather's autograph. One day he slipped his autograph book (without the money) in the pile of books, journals, notebooks, and slips of paper, so sure his grandfather wouldn't notice. Gandhi wasn't fooled. Arun had to pay 5 rupees just like everyone else, no exceptions! Arun learned a lot from his grandfather, and he eventually founded the M.K. Gandhi Institute for Nonviolence.

I'VE BEEN LOOKING FOR YOU

Many years ago, Father Joseph Brannigan, did some missionary work in the poor nation of Tanzania. One day in the chapel he saw a mother crying at the alter. Her baby was next to her. He asked why she was crying. She replied that her baby was dead. He could see the baby moving and said, "The child is not dead." The lady said, "But she will be soon because I have no money for her medicines." Father gave her some money. Several years later a woman came up to him and handed him some money. He asked the 'stranger' about the money. She replied, "I've been looking for you. I'm paying you back the money you gave me for my girl's medicine. She is alive and healthy." This story is adapted from the book, *Once Upon a Time in Africa*.

CHAPTER 5
TENACITY

"It's not that I'm so smart, it's just
that I stay with things longer."
—Albert Einstein

"Press on. Nothing in the world can take the
place of perseverance. Talent will not; nothing is
more common than unsuccessful men with talent.
Genius is almost a proverb. Education will not;
the world is full of educated derelicts. Persistence
and determination alone are omnipotent."
—Calvin Coolidge

ANIMAL TENACITY & HUMAN TENACITY

As I explore the topic of tenacity I seem to find more references
to animals than humans. We often hear of bulldog-tenacity, snap-
ping turtles that 'won't let go' and lost cats that travel hundreds of
miles to find their way home. In my previous books I've written
many stories about animals that were stubborn, determined, or
achieved amazing feats.

❖ A red-tailed hawk caught a copperhead snake. It killed the
    snake and was eating it when another copperhead, lying
    nearby, struck at the hawk. In the ensuing battle, the hawk

killed the second snake, but not before the snake had bitten the hawk in the neck. The hawk died between its two victims.

- ❖ A man caught a large catfish and hauled it to shore. When he cut it open he found inside several tiny fishes, a frog, old fish hooks, and a whole squirrel!

- ❖ Shrews must be constantly eating. Their digestive canals are so short that they have to eat twice their weight every twenty-four hours to survive. Shrews captured in the evening have been known to starve overnight.

- ❖ There's the story of a man who shot an eagle and found the dry skull of a weasel fixed by the jaws to his throat. It is believed that the eagle had attacked the weasel and the weasel turned and bit, tooth to neck, and nearly won. The weasel, even though dead did not let go and the eagle carried its dead body around for months, attached to the neck.

- ❖ A man had a pet squirrel. He kept it in his bedroom. One night the man placed 200 hickory nuts on his bureau. When he woke up he discovered that the squirrel had stored/hid them all, in shoes, in curtains, inside pants pockets, in flower pots, under the bed, and several other places!

- ❖ A scientist captured a Manx Shearwater (bird) at its nesting burrow in Wales and took it by plane across the Atlantic Ocean to Boston. A band was placed on one of its legs before being released. Although it had to fly over open sea, the bird headed straight for home, a distance of 3,200 miles, and arrived back at its burrow 12 days later.

- ❖ National Geographic News reported that a bar-tailed godwit flew non-stop, 7,145 miles from Alaska to New Zealand. It is the longest nonstop bird migration ever measured.

Animals need tenacity to survive. Most creatures in the wild spend the vast portion of their days, either looking for food to eat or trying to avoid being eaten themselves! In our world today, unfortunately, there are millions of humans operating in the survival mode. When they get up every morning they face poverty, famine, war, and violence in their neighborhoods. Most Americans are blessed to have their basic needs met so they have more time and energy to focus on personal goals, achievements, and dreams. So far in the *GOT GRIT?* Program we've discussed the importance of getting along with others, being responsible, and having integrity, but this final component, tenacity, is what separates the truly successful from the not-so-successful. It involves setting goals, developing plans, determination, delayed gratification, making sacrifices, overcoming adversities, eliminating excuses, setting priorities and being able to cope with a bit of fatigue and pain once in a while. Successful people soon become well aware of these terms that are associated with grit and tenacity: bravery, courage, doggedness, fortitude, guts, perseverance, spirit, stamina, staying power, and toughness. And don't forget, we should utilize our tenacity for three purposes: 1) to improve ourselves, 2) to help others, 3) to help make the world a better place. Let's get tenacious!

A TWELVE-STEP PLAN FOR BECOMING MORE TENACIOUS

1 **Have a goal.** What is your dream, your goal? Be realistic and optimistic; don't set the bar too low. The first step to achieving a goal is to write it down. Marla Runyan, the legally-blind American Olympic marathoner says, "If you don't have a dream, go get one. Write it down anywhere, on a small piece of paper or in your notebook. Just write it down, look at it every day, and remind yourself what you are working towards." Evangelist, Joyce Meyer, tells us, "A #2 pencil and a dream can take you anywhere." Make a personal commitment to pursue your goal **and** keep these two sayings always in your mind:

If you want something you've never had,
you must do something you've never done.

You don't get what you wish for;
you get what you work for.

2 **Visualize success.** Before you officially begin work on your goal, find some quiet time. Seek solitude to think about your goal, visualize succeeding, and consider praying or meditating. Then select a date to start and begin preparing for your journey. Abe Lincoln said, "If I have eight hours to chop a tree—I will spend six hours sharpening my axe."

You must 'see' your goal

Farmer Jones was sitting on the porch of his mountain cabin with his dog, Willie. Soon a young fox ran by. Willie saw it and took off howling. Neighborhood dogs, hearing Willie's barking, joined in. For over an hour all the dogs ran up and down the hills, howling and chasing. Jones watched the event. Soon all the dogs, except Willie, tuckered out and returned to their homes. Why did Willie keep going? He saw his goal, the fox. The other dogs never saw the goal, they participated in the chase but didn't know what they were looking for. You must see your goal before starting your chase.

3 **Be patient.** Seldom are dreams and goals accomplished quickly. In fact, author and motivational speaker, Po Bronson says, "Most dreams take ten years to mature." For instance, if you practice piano five hours every week for ten years, you'll end up practicing a total of 5,200 hours! You ought to be a pretty good piano player by then. Be patient. Theologian Charles Spurgeon reminds us, "By perseverance the snails reached the Ark."

4 **Step out of your comfort zone.** In his book, *The Dream Giver*, Dr. Bruce Wilkinson writes, "Your dream is always outside your comfort area." So many people have great plans, goals, and dreams but are not willing to change their daily routines. Are you ready to step out of your areas of comfort? In your pursuit you'll have to take risks, get up earlier, stay up later, turn off the television, get outside in the elements, move to a new town, change your diet, read more, get away from negative people, find new friends, and so on. Wilkinson stresses that fear and nervousness is normal when we step out of our comfort zones.

5 **Put your plan on paper.** What is a plan? It is a scheme or project. It is a guide or way of proceeding to make a change, usually for the better. Dr. William Glasser wrote the book, *Reality Therapy*, in which he describes a step-by-step process for changing behavior. Glasser stressed the importance of people writing plans to help them during the process of change. A good plan should contain a *what,* a *how,* and a *when.* What is your plan? How are you going to do it? When are you going to do it? Let's say your dream or goal is to write a children's book.

> **What:** To write a children's book about being kind to animals.

> **How:** Purchase writing material, work in my room, and ask family for cooperation (quiet time).

> **When:** I will write for two hours every Tuesday and Thursday night, 7-9pm. My goal is to have the manuscript sent off to the publisher by September 1.

After you write your plan, share it with others; let them know what you are up to. Select one person, family member or friend, to check up on you to make sure you are 'keeping your plan.' Keep a daily log or journal to record your progress.

Here is another point to consider when discussing plans. Keep in mind that your long-term goal will be comprised of many smaller goals. For instance, Josie wants to complete a tri-athlon one year from today; that's his long-range goal. During the year he'll have 365 small plans. Every morning he will need to set a daily goal (i.e., swim at the YMCA, go to the gym, read a book on biking, take a day off for rest, etc).

6 **Be strict!** If you are not strict with yourself, you won't make it. Stick with your plan and accept no excuses! As mentioned earlier in this book, in order to get "hooked" on positive activities or to make big changes in lifestyles, it will take at least a month of persistence. Get ready for possible fatigue or pain. Fatigue will come when trying to fit your new plan in to an already hectic schedule. You may have to get up an hour earlier or practice during lunch. Pain is a possibility. I believe that many people do not push themselves enough, once they start to feel a bit of pain or get 'uncomfortable,' they stop. Watch the faces of great athletes and you'll see pain. They are willing to push themselves to higher limits. Running the extra mile, swimming the extra laps, or practicing guitar an extra hour will reap many benefits!

Here is an example of the benefits of being strict. I'm a big fan of baseball, and I've noticed an interesting thing about hitters. If a minor league hitter gets only **two** hits for every ten at-bats, his batting average is .200; a .200 hitter seldom makes it to the major leagues. But, if a minor leaguer gets **three** hits out of ten (.300 avg.) he will more than likely make the majors and earn millions! Most .300 lifetime hitters enter the Baseball Hall of Fame. What a difference one more hit can make! Why do some players get three out-of-ten while others get only two? I'm sure for some it may be a God-given talent, but for others it may be their self-discipline and extra hours of practice.

7 **Keep gritty books and gritty friends close by.** Books can be great motivators, and they can teach us valuable lessons as we pursue our goals. Each year I read several books on running, fitness, the Olympics, and training tips. I enjoy biographies of successful runners. I also subscribe to four monthly running publications. Whatever your interest, read as much as you can about it. Good books and informative magazine articles will help keep you inspired. Also, besides reading more on your interests try to associate with others who have similar interests. C.S. Lewis said, "The next best thing to being wise oneself is to live in a circle of those who are." Join a yoga class, once a week bike with others, form a hiking club, start a quilting group, or get together and jam with other musicians.

8 **Create a ritual.** Having a set routine can 'jump-start' your daily pursuit. I always put on my 'lucky' hat just before heading out the door for my run. Some people repeat a motivational quote, chant, read a favorite scripture from the Bible, eat a granola bar, pet the dog, or say a prayer before working on their goals. I know a runner who places a dollar in a jar before each run. When the jar is full, she donates the money to the local animal shelter. Create your own unique ritual.

9 **Expect setbacks.** At one time or another everyone will encounter bumps in the roads and detours. Illness, injuries, moving, changing schools or jobs, financial problems, and family issues will hamper your progress at times. Bad things will happen, but be patient, press on, and be optimistic. Marathoner, Marla Runyan, who was diagnosed with Stargardt's disease, a juvenile form of macular degeneration, became legally blind at the age of nine says, "I think what I represent is *achieving* what you want in life. It's a matter of *attitude*. Some people have a negative attitude, and that's their disability."

10 **Celebrate your achievements.** When you are making progress, reward yourself. Buy a new CD, go on a picnic, buy an ice cream cone, or take a long afternoon nap. When my son Aaron and I are training for a marathon we closely monitor our calories, but on race day we stop at Dunkin' Donuts and purchase a dozen of our favorites. As soon as the 26.2 mile race is over, we open the box and devour!

11 **Don't let your dream fade. Make adjustments as needed. Get creative.** Instead of giving up, make some adjustments. If you don't complete your goal on time, add a few days, weeks, months, or another year! If you fail, step back, get creative and come up with another plan. David was Israel's most famous king. At one time he put together an elite group of warriors known as "David's Thirty." Hundreds of men desired to be part of this army, but David was very selective. Almost every one of his "thirty" was chosen because of his creative ability to use the bow and arrow and slingshot. Through hard work and tenacity they mastered the skill of handling their weapons either left or right-handed. The warriors who made the group did so thanks to their creativity and hard work.

12 **Select another dream.** After you've accomplished your goal, select another. Keep growing, no matter your age. Grandma Moses didn't start painting until she was 80 and completed more than 1,500 works before she died.

I have a good friend who likes to use the phrase, "Make it happen!" Whenever one of his students or athletes comes up with a great idea or needs money for a summer camp, he tells him or her, "Make it happen!" He places responsibility back on the children, letting them know that if they want it bad enough, they must take the lead. Do you have goals, dreams, or changes you wish to make in your life? Then, get tenacious and make it happen!

I'll end this chapter with one of my favorite stories about a young man who had a goal, encountered roadblocks, got creative and didn't give up. This story comes from my book, *Quips, Quotes, & Quick Starters*.

THE HOUSE OF CHICKEN FEATHERS

One of the world's most well-known humanitarians, Albert Schweitzer said, "Even if it's a little thing, do something for those who have need of help, something for which you get no pay but the privilege of doing it. " Helping others is important, but it isn't always simple or easy. A kind missionary in Peking, China one hundred and fifty years ago encountered numerous problems when he showed kindness to the poor. It would have been easy for him to give up. Instead, he got very creative and his efforts paid off.

Harland Sinclair left his home in London and traveled to China to serve as a missionary. When he walked the streets in Peking, he was shocked to see so many poor and homeless sleeping out in the cold. He set a personal goal to do all he could to help them have a safe, warm place to spend the evenings.

Harland eventually found an old abandoned warehouse to use for his plan. He covered the dirt floor with a thick layer of chicken feathers. Every night the poor arrived by the hundreds: adults and children. The missionary charged visitors a penny and each was given a blanket to borrow for the night. After a few days Harland had a big problem; the poor failed to leave the borrowed blankets behind. Obviously he was upset but he wasn't going to give up. He had to come up with a new plan.

Along with the help of local government officials, a new strategy was initiated. A huge blanket was suspended from the ceiling by a system of cables. When the poor arrived at night and were settled in, a bell rang and pulleys slowly lowered the massive blanket down over the visitors and the chicken feathers. Holes were cut into the blanket so the people could stick their heads out and breathe. At seven in the morning the bell rang and the pulleys lifted the blanket off the sleepers. Hundreds of poor headed back to the streets after a good night's rest.

Harland's persistence and tenacity worked! Years later he left China with a good feeling knowing that his work had a positive impact on the needy.

PART THREE

GRIT:
How Do You
Pass It On?

CHAPTER 6
PASSING IT ON TO OTHERS

"What do we live for if not to make
life less difficult for each other?"
—George Eliot

"Therefore, encourage one another and
build up each other as in fact you are doing."
—1 Thessalonians 5:11

"He could have added fortune to fame, but caring for neither,
he found happiness and honor in being helpful to the world."
—epitaph on George Washington Carver's grave

WHAT'S YOUR GQ?

If I've done a decent job so far in this book, I've been able to convince readers that their GQ (Grit Quotient) is more important than their IQ. What's your GQ? Are you mastering the four components of the GRIT Program: Getting along with others, showing responsibility, having integrity and being tenacious? If you feel good about your GQ, then it is time for you to move on to the next and most important step, passing GRIT on to others. Once again, you can't pass it on to others if you don't have any! Following are several strategies, ideas, tips, and thoughts that will help you with this very important task. Good luck!

GRIT TIPS: PASSING IT ON TO OTHERS

1 **Model GRIT.** This is extremely important, especially when working with young people. Modeling grit falls into three categories. First, do others witness you being kind, responsible, in control of your emotions, persevering, and taking good care of your health (i.e. diet, exercise)? Second, do your students, friends, co-workers, and/or family members see you setting and achieving personal goals such as pursuing a degree, losing weight, mastering a new skill, writing a book, or learning to play a musical instrument? I don't think people realize the positive impact we have on others when they see us striving to set and achieve personal goals. Third, I believe it is very important that people see us helping others. We should never be boastful or prideful, but when others, old and young, see us volunteer, donate money, or deliver meals to the poor, it often encourages them to do the same. What are you doing for others?

2 **Tea for three.** Get your day off to a good start by having tea or coffee, breakfast, and good conversation with these three: **God**: Consider a few minutes of prayer to ask for guidance in order to help yourself and others. **Self:** Ask yourself, "What are my goals and objectives for today?" Repeat a couple positive affirmations. **Significant other:** Share your thoughts, daily goals with someone you love. Encourage him or her to have a productive day. If you live alone, it is okay to talk to your dog or cat.

3 **Be kind.** Sometimes this can be very difficult, but we must model it. If people are rude to us and we return the rudeness, what have we accomplished? I can remember times when people said unkind things to me and I would get upset and say something unkind in return. Afterwards I never felt good about it. Spiritual writer, Hugh Prather says, "Sometimes I think all we are learning in life is that we are happy when we are kind, and unhappy when we are not. We resist the lesson because it's so simple it's insulting."

4 **Have tough skin.** Occasionally you'll encounter someone who will question your motives when you try to help him or her. These people may also say some hurtful things. Have tough skin and don't take it personally. Often they may be dealing with personal issues and attempt to pass their pain on to you. They aren't really angry with you; you may be a safe or convenient target at which to vent. Also, realize that the more things you do to help people, the more you open yourself to the criticism from others. For instance, if you organize a dinner at church to raise money to help the homeless and you spend hundreds hours of hard doing it, come Monday morning the first member of the congregation to go to the kitchen may start fussing about you because there was one dirty dish in the sink! Here is a personal example. Every year I coordinate after-school clubs for students. I recruit leaders, find spaces to meet, buy supplies, print schedules, get permission slips, and so on. I do the clubs for the kids. I don't have to but I know how valuable they are. Every year I get few negative comments from parents and students about the clubs. They may be upset because some clubs have a limited number of participants or because I didn't have a certain club one year such as soccer or poetry. When I get a rude phone call I often think, "I'm not getting paid for this; I'm doing it for kids! If I wasn't doing the clubs, I wouldn't be getting these calls!" Have tough skin and press on.

5 **Beware of the sloth.** On your mission you'll meet up with people with unusual temperaments and personalities. They have little or no desire to change and appear almost impossible to arouse. In his book, *Sabbatical Journey*, Henri Nouwen refers to these individuals as "slothful." He notes, "I can see how hard— yes, impossible—it is to preach to people who are slothful because nothing really matters to them. They don't get excited about a beautiful thought, a splendid idea, or an encouraging perspective, nor do they become indignant about ugly words, sordid ideas, or destructive viewpoints. Evelyn Waugh, according to Ralph C. Wood, once called sloth the besetting late-modern sin. I believe Waugh is right. It seems to be the sin of a spoiled generation, for whom nothing really matters." Nouwen goes on to discourage us from giving up on these challenging people. He writes, "I realize that much of what I want to do is to help people break out of their prison of sloth and become engaged in making the world a better place. I am trying so hard to do this that I'm criticized for overemphasizing, exaggerating, and getting too excited." Be persistent. Don't give up. You may not be able to change every sloth into a greyhound, but you might be able to at least get them a little bit excited about changing.

6 **Take risks.** Don't be afraid to take an occasional risk. The words "do not be afraid" appear 366 times in the Bible. Author Anais Nin says, "And the day came when the risk it took to remain tightly closed in a bud was more painful than the risk it took to bloom." As you assist people, you have to encourage them to take risks and step out of their comfort zones. Olympic coach, Percy Cerutty said, "You only grow as a human being if you're outside your comfort zone."

7 **Inspire or motivate?** Is there a difference between the two words? Is it better to inspire or motivate others? When people see me running in the rain, do a few of them become inspired or motivated to start a new fitness routine? Lance Secretan's article in the July 2006 issue of *Spirituality & Health* gave me a new perspective on these two terms. He wrote:

> *We have confused motivation with inspiration, even though these two concepts are quite different. Motivation means to provide a motive, to induce, incite, impel. It's based on fear. If I say I'll give you a bonus when you make your budget or sales quota—and not, if you don't—it's essentially a bribe. Now you are afraid you won't make it. Fear has become the motivating factor......Look at the word "inspiration." It comes from the Latin 'spirare,' spirit. To inspire is to infuse with an encouraging or exalting influence; to animate......Motivation and inspiration don't have a lot in*

common. Inspiration isn't about me, it's a gift to you that comes from my love for you and my desire to serve you in some way. If you've ever had a great coach or mentor, you know that this person inspired you out of love for you....Motivation is about me. Inspiration is about you. Motivation is about fear. Inspiration is about love.

Many people try to motivate others because it makes them look good. A teacher might say, "Hey, I got ten kids to improve their math scores! My motivational strategies worked." Were the students really motivated by the teacher or by the fear of not passing? Maybe the teacher should focus on building a strong, caring relationship with his students so they become **inspired** to improve. Students may think, "Hey, Mr. Carrington really cares about us and wants us to succeed, so let's work harder."

8 **Be a 'great' listener.** One of the best ways to help others make positive changes in their lives is to listen to them, **really** listen! Let them talk, share their frustrations, and it is all right to show empathy. We all feel better when people truly listen to us. How are your listening skills? Larry Crabb and Dan Allender, in the book *Encouragement: The Key to Caring*, write, "Active listeners require concentrated effort. It notices facial grimaces, slumped shoulders, quiet sighs, lifeless tones of voice, and moist eyes. Sensitive listeners respond to comments with words that convey an interest in hearing more sentences that open the door to information."

9 **Encourage optimism.** Your optimism can rub off. If Aubrey believes that you think she can do it, she just might!

10 **Acknowledge their special gifts and talents.** I believe everyone is born with special gifts and talents, but often these treasures are wasted, unused. Let others know that you are cognizant of their strengths. A few simple acknowledgements can do wonders.

Maurice, you have a great voice. Consider joining the choir.

Jose, you sure can run! Have you ever thought about trying out for the cross country team?

Ruby, these poems are great. You ought to submit them for publication.

Sharon, you've got the patience of Job. I wish I had that gift.

Alex, I've been watching you. You've got great leadership skills.

Whenever you are working with others be sure to concentrate on their strengths. There is a Maori saying, "Highlight my strengths and my weaknesses will disappear."

11 **Greetings & Good-byes.** Take time to really get to know your friends, co-workers, students, and neighbors. Find out about their hobbies, interests, gifts, talents, pets, family members, where they go to school or church, and other tidbits of information. Once you know more about them, then you can make greetings and good-byes more meaningful. For example, instead of saying, "Hello, John," say, "Hello, John, how's your running going? Got any races lined up?" If you see Louise say, "Hi, I've heard that you are speaking to the youth group. What's the topic?"

Other examples:

Good morning Celeste. How's that term paper coming?

Hey, Ian. I saw in the paper your team lost to Hayford. What happened?

Good morning Mike. What's on your agenda today?

Hello Benny, nice to see you. Added anymore arrowheads to your collection?

Most people enjoy answering questions about their hobbies, interests, and so on. I love it when someone asks me things like, "How many miles did you run last week?" or "What was your time in Saturday's 5k?" By asking about activities in their lives, instead of the basic, "Hello," shows you are truly interested and care about them. A few "inquiring words" can be very inspiring.

Get more creative with your good-byes as well. Make them positive and make some of them open-ended, leaving the recipient with a possible plan of action. Instead of saying, "I hope you have a nice day." try, "Have a productive day." I always liked the positive good-byes used by Robert Schuler, Jr. and Rich Mullins. Schuler, from California's famous Crystal Cathedral doesn't say, "May God bless you." He says, "God **is** blessing you." The late contemporary Christian music writer and singer, Rich Mullins ended visits with, "Be God's."

Here are some examples of open-ended good-byes:

*See ya, John. How many pages of
Harry Potter are you going to read tonight?*

*Good-bye, Luke. How many laps
are you going to swim tonight?*

*Good luck. I'll see you next week and
I want you have some good news for me.*

Good night. I hope you think about what I suggested.

12 **Offer challenges.** Sometimes I'll joke with a student and say, "I bet you can't do that." Those simple words make him want to prove me wrong. Long range challenges are better. If Teresa tells you, "I'd like to run a 5k race in the spring," you could reply, "You can do it and when (not if) you do, I'll treat you to a movie and dinner." When Dottie says, "I hope I can sell 100 boxes of Girl Scout cookies," say "When you do, I'll shave my beard."

13 **Park the helicopter.** Earlier in the book we talked about helicopter parents who are constantly hovering over their children, always bailing them out and not letting them "fall on their faces" once in a while. If we really want others to acquire GRIT, one of the best things we can do is to let them suffer natural and logical consequences. How will Mandy learn responsibility if dad always pays her over-due book fees at the library? Are you really helping your friend Rick by covering for him when he's constantly late for work? Remember, one of the best ways to help others grow is, don't always help them!

14 **Eliminate the word 'why' when people are not responsible.** I discussed this issue earlier in the book. Let's review. Whenever a person doesn't fulfill a required or requested task and we ask "why," we are inviting her to come up with an excuse to justify her lack of responsibility. If you witness your daughter Molly hitting her brother Henry and you ask, "Why did you hit him?" she'll say something like, "Well, he hit me first," or "He called me a name." Rarely is there a valid reason for hitting. Your best response would be to say, "I saw you hit Henry. You know hitting is not allowed in this house, now go to your room and we'll discuss it later." Try to get in the habit of using the word 'what' instead of 'why.' Instead of saying, "Minnie, why haven't you done the dishes," say, "Minnie what chore was to be finished by now?" By using the word 'what' you are placing responsibility back on the child, and you're not letting him come up with excuses. Dr. William Glasser said, "Parents who really love their children don't accept excuses." If your co-worker promised to turn in his records by noon and he hasn't, don't ask, "Why haven't turned in your records?" Instead, "Where are your records? You said you would have them to me by noon." Gritty people rarely use excuses. They accept responsibility for their actions; they don't blame others. My running buddies will never hear me say, "I didn't run today because it was raining or it was too cold." Don't tolerate excuses.

15 **Don't worry about balance.** Psychologists and researchers, Peter Doskoch and Carlin Flora, note, "It's impossible to be outstanding at everything—there simply aren't enough hours in a day for the requisite practice. 'Except for a few renaissance men and women, most people who have made important contributions to art, science, and the humanities have worked long and hard in one particular area,' notes Joseph Renzulli. 'So I often say to parents, 'If your children are doing something that they have a strong interest in and they are excelling, don't worry whether or not they are well balanced.'"

16 **Be there!** One of the most effective tools for nurturing GRIT is to be present at special activities and events that involve your family, friends, and students. If your son has a soccer game, be there! If your daughter is winning an award at the science fair, be there! I know it's impossible to attend every event, game, or ceremony, but strive to get to as many as you can. My wife tries her best to attend activities at various churches when her friends are being recognized. I've traveled many miles to watch my fellow runners compete. Early in my teaching career I discovered the power of going to see my students play in their sporting events. What great feelings I experienced at baseball fields when my students looked up and saw me there.

17 **Be careful with praise.** We've got to reduce the number of "praise-junkies" out there. Instead of praising children for their intelligence or accomplishments, recognize their effort. Don't say, "Jill you are so smart, you got a 100 on that test!" Change your comments to, "Jill you worked hard! You must be proud of yourself." It is important to let kids know we are aware of their positive behaviors, but they don't always need a sticker or a "good job!" shout. Rather than saying, "Bruno, I'm proud of you for sharing with your little brother," try "Bruno I noticed you sharing with your little brother." Remember, a little praise is ok, but don't overdo it. Too much praise can sound phony and become less sincere. When complimenting adults, use specific praise instead of general praise. Instead of, "Martha you're a good secretary," say, "Martha, I greatly admire the way you always remain so calm when things get hectic in the office; I'd go bonkers!" People tend to remember specific praise more than general praise.

18 Create a personal foundation. Keep a large jar or piggy bank on your desk. Whenever you have some spare change or a few extra dollars drop them in the container. This will become your own personal 'Foundation.' Name it after you. I call mine the Tom Carr Foundation. After you accumulate a decent amount donate it to someone or to a charity. Your Foundation could provide a summer scholarship for Jimmy to go to band camp. You might consider giving to Food for the Poor or the Red Cross. If you have children, provide them with containers and encourage them to create their own "Mini-Foundation."

19 Be a Gritty Storyteller. Everyone seems to enjoy hearing a good story, especially young people. Practice being a good storyteller and focus on true stories about gritty individuals. I love telling stories to students, and I've discovered that they learn more from my true stories than they do from regular lessons or lectures. I strongly recommend telling true stories about successful people. Many children read too much fiction, watch too much 'exaggerated' television, and play so many animated video games that they have trouble distinguishing between what is real or isn't real. My older students know that my stories are true. With very young children I do use a few fables, fairy tales, and fictional stories. Adults appreciate good stories. I've attended many boring workshops and heard numerous dull sermons, but when the presenters say, "Let me tell you a story," my ears perk up. Powerful stories can trigger emotions. Discipline expert and author Marvin Marshall says, "Logic prompts people to think. Emotions prompt people to act. If you want people to remember what you teach, touch an emotional chord by painting a picture or telling a story. There is a greater chance of the learning staying in long-term memory using these approaches than when the lesson just focuses on information itself."

20 Write letters or notes. Never underestimate the power of a quick note or a short letter of appreciation or thanks. Hand-write your "thanks" on a card, note, or piece of paper and deliver it. Also, send letters of congratulations, letters of encouragement, and simple letters that say, "Have a great day." Everyone enjoys getting good mail. A kind letter in one's mailbox can do wonders to lift spirits and lead him or her along the gritty trail to success.

21 **Talk about heroes.** Here is a fun activity to try with others of all ages. I learned this from a great sermon one Sunday. The pastor told us that we should all have four heroes: a Biblical hero, a historical hero, a personal hero, and a present day hero. I selected, David, Abraham Lincoln, my father, and Lance Armstrong. After your friends or students write down their choices, ask them to share and give reasons why they chose those people. We all need heroes!

22 **Just say, "Thank you."** Here is a tough habit to break. Have you noticed that almost every time you thank someone or say something positive, he comes back with a nice comment about you? You might say, "Mitch, your solo was great!" Then he replies, "Thanks. I thought you did fantastic as well." My belief is if someone compliments you, thanks you, or acknowledges your effort, they are giving you a gift. The best way to accept the gift is to simply say, "Thank you." Let them enjoy giving you their gift. Don't diminish their special moment by quickly giving them a gift in return.

23 **When they say, "That's not fair!"** As we try our best to help others, we'll hear people complain, blame others, or say, "That's not fair." I usually respond with, "Yes, sometimes things aren't fair, but we have to move." Often I'll joke and say, "Take a can of 'suck it up' and get over it!" Once in a while I'll do a lesson with my students on the "It's not fair," topic. I'll start by asking, "How would you feel if your parents named you Loser? Would that be fair?" Of course all the kids reply, "No way!" Then I tell them this true story.

Winner & Loser

In 1958, Mr. Robert Lane lived in New York City. He and his wife had a baby boy. Mr. Lane saw something 'special' in the baby's eyes so he named him Winner. How could a kid be unsuccessful with a name like that? Three years later the Lanes had another boy and for some strange reason, Mr. Lane named the boy Loser. So how did Winner and Loser do in life? Check this out! Winner accumulated a lengthy criminal record including three dozen arrests for burglary, domestic violence, trespassing, resisting arrest, and other illegal activities. Loser went on to prep school, graduated from Lafayette College, and joined the New York Police Department where he was a detective and, eventually, a sergeant.

24 **Be a coach, mentor, or group leader.** Do you **really** want to help our youth to succeed? Then consider finding a couple hours a week to coach a team, be a Boy or Girl Scout leader, head up a chess club or book club. How about mentoring or tutoring?

25 **Ask, "Got GRIT?"** Ask that question often to adults and children. As I walk up and down the halls at school I ask kids, "Got GRIT?" They almost always say "Yes!" Then they return the question, "Mr. Carr, got GRIT?" If I come across a friend or co-worker who is struggling I'll ask them the question.

CHAPTER 7
HOW TO IMPLEMENT THE "GOT GRIT?" PROGRAM IN YOUR SCHOOL / CLASSROOM

GROWING GRITTY STUDENTS

VERY IMPORTANT: Please make sure you read the previous six chapters before you consider implementing the GOT GRIT? Program in your school or classroom.

It is time to make some major changes in education in order to **truly** prepare our students for the future. Education leaders and government programs such as No Child Left Behind continue to push math, reading, and technology at the expense of science, social students, the arts, physical education, and social skills. Yes, our young people need to improve in math and reading, but if you take a close look at recent research you'll discover that there are more important skills needed in order to get **and** keep jobs. I tell my students that the number one reason people can't keep a job is they can't get along with co-workers or their supervisors. Employers now days are attempting to let educators know that potential employees need some hard skills, but more importantly they need soft skills, also known as people skills. As you read on you'll find that the GOT GRIT? Program focuses more on soft skills as the best avenue on the road to success.

Before I list the steps for implementing this program in your school or classroom, keep these thoughts in your head.

❖ The U.S. Department of Labor informs us that within the next five to ten years, two-thirds of the job openings will not require a four-year degree. Our students will need at least a high school diploma, a two year-degree, technical school and/or on the job training **and** good soft skills!

❖ We should do all we can to get students to stay in school and graduate. Once they graduate then there are options for further higher education. In our country today there are colleges "begging" for high school graduates. As long as a student has a diploma, there is a college somewhere that will accept him. Obviously, if a young person wishes to go on to a more competitive college or university, he must keep up his grades and take advanced classes.

❖ Employers continue to stress the importance of soft skills. I'm not so sure how people skills got to be known as **soft** skills because they are **hard** to teach. Just the reverse is true also. Hard skills are not as **hard** to teach as **soft** skills. Dennis Coates, CEO of Performance Support Systems, Inc. says, "Hard skills are technical or administrative procedures related to an organization's core business. Examples include machine operator, computer protocols, safety standards, financial procedures and sales administration. These skills are typically easy to observe, quantify and measure. They're easy to train because most of the time the skill sets are brand new to the learner and no unlearning is involved." Soft skills involve a lot of unlearning. It isn't easy to help someone change attitude, behavior, and personality! I hope you agree that most of the time it is easier to teach Joseph how to use a keyboard than to teach him to control his anger, a very important soft skill.

❖ What kinds of soft skills are employers looking for? Lori Kocon, a human resource expert, lists her top ten needed soft skills:

—Strong work ethic

—Positive attitude

—Good communication skills

—Time management abilities

—Problem-solving skills

—Acting as a team player

—Self-confidence

—Ability to accept and learn from criticism

—Flexibility and adaptability

—Working well under pressure

Following are several strategies to help you get the GOT GRIT? PROGRAM started in your school or individual classroom. The program can be adapted to all levels K-12. Remember as you read the strategies, you'll see there is more of a focus on soft skills than hard skills. A person can have great hard skills, but if she is weak in soft skills, she'll struggle.

IMPLEMENTING THE *GOT GRIT?* PROGRAM IN SCHOOL

1 **Review your Mission Statement.** Does your school's Mission Statement reflect the importance of both soft and hard skills? During the past few years I've been able to visit many schools throughout the country. When I visit a school, I often look for its Mission Statement. Here is my favorite.

MISSION STATEMENT
Realizing that no learning can take place without self-love, we are spiritually united in providing a warm, nurturing climate devoted to building self-esteem and acceptance among all components of the triad: student, parent, and faculty. With this background students will be equipped to face an ever-changing environment, confident of their ability to contribute positively to society.
—Melrose Park Elementary School
Lake City, Florida   1999

2 **Review school and class rules.** Once again, do they stress the importance of people skills? Keep your rules "short & sweet." At Cameron Park Elementary in Hillsborough, North Carolina we came up with a code rather than a long list of rules.

The Cameron Park Code:
It's never ok to hurt anyone's body, anyone's feelings, anyone's property or anyone's learning.

3 **Model GRIT:** Does the staff model the four components of GRIT?: Getting along with others, showing responsibility, having integrity, and being tenacious.

4 **Educate the students about the program.** Let students know what 'true' GRIT is and why it is important. Explain the four components.

5 **Promote the program.**

❖ Have students make and hang "GOT GRIT?" posters throughout the school.

❖ Order "GOT GRIT?" stickers. Stickers can be placed on desks as a constant reminder to work hard. I place stickers on all my correspondence with students, parents and teachers. I want as many people as possible to see the words, GOT GRIT?

❖ Order pens and pencils with the GOT GRIT? on them.

❖ Purchase some plastic yellow hard hats (construction hats). Wear one occasionally as a reminder to students to work hard. Since the hats are inexpensive (50 cents), you can let kids wear them as well. Let the hard hats be visible in your classroom at all times. You can schedule a "GOT GRIT? Week" near the end of the school year to encourage students to finish strong. At my school we did this and all adults at the school wore yellow hats that week!

❖ Create a GRIT Hall of Fame for those students who have made great progress and model GRIT.

❖ Instead of awarding good citizenship, consider awarding GRIT.

❖ Promote the program on your school's television show. Have a student wear the yellow hard hat when making his presentation.

❖ Get in the habit of using the question, "Got GRIT?" When a student starts to struggle, complain, or give up, ask, "Got GRIT?"

❖ Place information about the program in your parent newsletters.

6 **Post gritty quotes throughout the school.** Come up with ten quotes about working hard, not giving up, and getting along with others. After a while the students will know them well. Here are a few of my favorite quotes. I use them often in my class lessons.

If you want something you've never had,
you must do something you've never done.
(Tom Carr)

You don't get what you wish for
you get what you work for.
(Anonymous)

Responsible people are happy people.
Happy people are responsible people.
(Marvin Marshall)

It takes grit to be fit.
(Tom Carr)

The key ingredient in the formula for success
is the ability to get along with others.
(Theodore Roosevelt)

The more concerned we become over the things
we can't control, the less we will do
with the things we can control.
(John Wooden)

To be bored is an insult to oneself.
(Jules Renard)

Gold medals aren't really made of gold.
They're made of sweat, determination,
and a hard to find alloy called guts.
(Dan Gable)

Success is a choice.
(Rick Pitino)

7 **Teach responsibilities, procedures, and mastering arenas on a regular basis.** Throughout the school day students travel through several arenas (bus, halls, cafeteria, media center, playground, bathroom, and so on), and they must know how to behave in these varied settings. Teachers should have students practice classroom and school-wide procedures often, and they must be consistent when monitoring the procedures and rules. Do your students know the procedures? I got the following list from one of Marvin Marshall's monthly newsletters. It comes from Serrano Intermediate School of Lake Forest in Orange County, California.

DO YOUR STUDENTS KNOW:

How to enter your classroom quietly?

What they should do right after the bell rings?

How to pass up assignments?

Where and how to turn in late work?

How to distribute handouts you give them?

How to retrieve their graded work?

When to sharpen a pencil or get a tissue?

When to request to use the bathroom?

When to talk?

How to participate in classroom discussions?

How to behave during a test?

When to get a dictionary or other classroom resource?

What to do if they don't have a pencil or paper?

When to dig in their backpacks?

How to keep backpacks out of walkways?

How and when to move around the room?

How to take, use, and return classroom supplies?

How to appropriately use classroom equipment?

How to throw away trash without disturbing others?

When and how to work quietly?

When and how to clean up work area?

What to do if they finish an assignment early?

When they can read leisurely?

How to behave during a classroom video and audio?

How to record assignments in their planner?

What information is available on your webpage?

How to work cooperatively in groups?

Evacuation plans during an emergency?

How to work with a substitute teacher?

How to exit the classroom at the end of the period?

I find it very interesting that almost every thing on this list can be considered a soft skill.

8 **Teach social skills.** Teachers and counselors need to work closely to teach important social skills. This can be done on a daily basis within the classroom. Teachers can provide lessons, model good social skills, use teachable moments and conduct discussions on which types of social skills are needed as children move from one arena to another. Counselors can provide small group counseling and social skills groups for students who need extra help.

9 Teach and model Character Education, but be careful!

I've touched on Character Education earlier in the book. Do children need to master good character traits? Of course! But we must be careful how we do it. I have a theory: *Character education is caught, not taught, nor bought.* I truly believe that most schools can do a good job teaching character without spending much money at all! I've visited numerous schools throughout the country that have spent thousands of dollars on videos, books, and posters. All the posters hanging on the wall, banners draped across the front door, and several signs noting: *This week's character trait is trust,* doesn't necessarily mean that true character education is being taught. I will never forget the day I visited one of those schools that had all kinds of character paraphernalia hanging on the walls. As I entered the building, I could here an adult yelling at a kid. There was a teacher totally humiliating a middle-schooler in front many students and other faculty members. As she continued her verbal assault, I looked above her heard and saw a beautiful, and probably expensive, poster that read: **RESPECT OTHERS.**

When implementing a character education program at your school, please give the following suggestions some consideration.

❖ Adult modeling is crucial. Students need to see educators being kind, resolving conflicts in positive ways, and modeling the character traits that they teach.

❖ Don't show a character education film or read a book to your students without following up with a discussion.

❖ Teachable moments can be very effective. For instance, if some of your students were showing poor sportsmanship on the playground, call a time-out, form a circle, and talk.

❖ When you witness good character, be careful with praise. Acknowledge their actions, but do not always praise. Instead of saying, "I'm so proud of you for helping Mr. Bell pick up the mess," say, "I saw you helping Mr. Bell." Remember, we don't need to raise more "praise junkies." We want children to help him because it is the right thing to do, not because they expect praise or goodies.

❖ Avoid character education programs that provide tangible "reinforcers." Let me say it again, much research done by experts like Marvin Marshall, William Glasser, and Alfie Kohn tell us that these programs may appear to be working for a short time. In other words, if you pass out tokens to students for good character, you'll notice behavior improve for a while, but when you remove the "goodies," they usually revert back to their negative behaviors. Many of the Julies, Jimmys, Henrys, and Jareds were *acting* good in order to get their rewards! Our goal is to get children to do the right thing because it is the right thing to do, not because they expect a treat! In his book, *Unconditional Parenting*, Alfie Kohn writes, "We have two studies showing that children who are frequently rewarded or praised tend to be less generous and helpful than other kids—and the effect is more pronounced for the kids who were rewarded or praised for being generous or helpful." He also notes, "The more you reward kids for doing something, the more they come to lose interest in whatever they had to do to get the reward."

❖ Don't spend a lot of money on posters, videos, and other materials. Consider giving more money for art supplies, musical instruments, nutritional snacks, summer camp scholarships, or after-school clubs.

10 **Use what, not why.** Have the staff sign a contract agreeing not to ask "Why?" when a child is not being responsible.

11 **Evaluate the purpose and amount of homework you assign.** Do children need homework every night? How much time should they spend on homework? Do all kids go home to houses with good lighting, heat or air-conditioning, encyclopedias, two parents, and a quiet place to work? What do kids need more, two hours of homework or two hours of outside play? If you give too much homework does it interfere with their sports, clubs, church, and quality family time? What does the most recent research tell us about homework?

12 **Discuss health issues with students.** Gritty kids need to know the importance of getting enough sleep, eating nutritious meals, and exercising. Teachers can make sure their kids get outside, drink a lot of water, and eat healthy snacks.

13 **Provide after-school clubs.** Teachers realize how important it is to get young people involved in positive after-school activities. Our most successful students are busy with sports, clubs, band, chorus, and so on. Students who do not get involved in these activities tend to become behavior problems and they are more likely to drop out. Elementary schools can do much to get children excited about extra-curricular activities by providing clubs, either during regular school hours of after school. Faculty members should be encouraged to head up clubs based on their personal likes or skills. Some clubs could meet two or three times while others could be year-long. Clubs may provide a spark and motivate children to pursue new interests. Every year at my school I get many teachers and parents to volunteer to lead clubs such as chess, wrestling, soccer, quilting, poetry, drawing, storytelling, etiquette, drama, card trading, running, jump rope, aerobics, yoga, and arts & crafts. Approximately 70% of the students in grades 2-5 participate in at least one of these after-school clubs. Middle school and high school teachers need to find time to get involved with after-school activities once in a while. They can lead a club, coach, or provide extra academic help such as tutoring.

14 **Create a GRIT Report Card.** One idea to help young people understand the importance of having GRIT is to create a GRIT Report Card. Get creative and devise one. You can grade each child at the end of each grading period. On the card give a score of A, B, C, D for each of the four components: getting along with others, showing responsibility, having integrity, and being tenacious. Be sure to provide comments, suggestions, etc. If a student gets many A's and B's on the GRIT Report Card, he or she is bound to be successful. Could a student's GRIT Report Card be a better predictor of his future success than his regular school report card?

15 **Tell them gritty stories.** Find **true** stories about people who had grit, overcame setbacks, had determination, and perseverance. There are several examples in Chapters 1 and 4.

16 **Organize a GRIT Crew.** Racecar drivers have a pit crew; gritty schools need a GRIT Crew. Select a small number of students who meet regularly with an advisor to evaluate the GOT GRIT? Program.

17 **Provide parent education.** As you implement the GOT GRIT? Program keep parents involved. Place articles in your class or school newsletter and on the school's webpage. Schedule a Parent Coffee Hour to explain the program and share information from this book. Here are three suggested titles for your gatherings:

Ten Tips for Raising Your Child's GQ (Grit Quotient)

Raising Gritty Kids

How to Nurture Your Child's Gritty Nature

18 **Invite Bob the Builder.** I enjoy dressing up as the cartoon character Bob the Builder. I wear a yellow hard hat and don a tool belt and visit classrooms. Bob is a very optimistic guy as he often says, "We can fix it." Even the older students get a kick out of seeing Bob. During my visits I tell the students that each tool in my belt has something to do with GRIT. The hammer represents tenacity; you have to keep pounding until the nail is in the wood. The level represents integrity. We often use the term 'level' when talking about honesty. We say, "Are you on the level?" or, "Are you being level with me?" Bob's keys represent responsibility. His blueprints outline his goals.

Acquiring GRIT is difficult. It will take much endurance. I'll finish this book with a poem that paints a perfect picture of hanging in there, having GRIT, and not giving up. The poem is based on the writer's childhood, growing up in the south during the 1950's and 60's.

Finding Endurance

I couldn't sleep all night,

90 degrees at midnight

and no air conditioning or

fan to create a breeze.

The next morning I'm standing out in the garden

picking butterbeans,

my back is tired

but mother's depending on me.

Later, I walk with my younger brother and sister

from the store, almost a mile from home

carrying a carton of soft drinks

stopping to rest…down on our knees.

Under the tobacco barn

working for five dollars a day,

waiting for a break, waiting for lunch,

waiting for dusk when I get my pay.

I'm not even 12 years old.

City kids don't know I exist,

they woke up late in the day,

spent the day at the pool,

played with their Barbies and Kens,

bought an ice cream bar from the ice cream man,

and then sat in their air-conditioned family rooms watching T.V.,

went to the movies,

or went swimming at the pool.,

while I was hoeing corn,

feeding the hogs,

and pulling up weeds,

mowing the yard,

working hard.

What's in it for me?

Homemade ice cream on special days,

working side by side with my family each day,

a new bike I bought with my own pay,

and I find endurance along the way.

—by Paula Stanley
from the book, *Finding Endurance*

About the Author

Tom Carr is a counselor, educational consultant, author and storyteller who lives in Hillsborough, North Carolina. He received his Master's Degree from Syracuse University. Tom is a National Certified Counselor and a Licensed Professional Counselor with thirty years experience as a teacher and counselor. He is the president and founder of Carr Counseling and Consultation, Inc. He has authored several books and presented over 400 workshops throughout the United States and Canada. To learn more about Tom, go to his website: www.tomcarrcounseling.com.

Other Books by Tom Carr

Keeping Love Alive in the Family
(out of print)

A Parents Blueprint
(out of print)

131 Creative Strategies for Reaching
Children with Anger Problems

141 Creative Strategies for Reaching
Adolescents with Anger Problems

When All Else Fails

Monday Morning Messages

Innovative Strategies for Unlocking Difficult Children

Every Child has a Gift

Return to the Land: The Search for Compassion

Guidance Giveaways

Quips, Quotes, and Quick Starters

*Tom's books can be purchased from
www.youthlightbooks.com*